REAL ESTATE MATH

REAL ESTATE MATH

All the Math Salespersons
and Brokers Need to Know

NEW YORK

Copyright © 2008 LearningExpress, LLC.

All rights reserved under International and Pan-American Copyright Conventions.
Published in the United States by LearningExpress, LLC., New York.

Library of Congress Cataloging-in-Publication Data:

Real estate math.
    p. cm.
  ISBN: 978-1-57685-631-4
1. Real estate business—Mathematics. I. LearningExpress (Organization)
  HF5695.5.R3R43 2008
  333.3301'513—dc22
                2007038879

ISBN: 978-1-57685-631-4

Printed in the United States of America

9 8 7 6 5 4 3 2 1

First Edition

For more information or to place an order, contact LearningExpress at:
    55 Broadway
    8th Floor
    New York, NY 10006

Or visit us at:
    www.learnatest.com

CONTENTS

INTRODUCTION

WHY REAL ESTATE PROFESSIONALS NEED MATH

Welcome! You are about to take a mathematical walk through the world of real estate. It's not the first thing most of us think of when we consider joining the profession as a salesperson or broker, but it is an essential skill. Salespeople and brokers need to be able to quickly (sometimes on the spot):

- calculate the mathematical pros and cons of comparables
- determine what that bit of extra square footage is worth
- prequalify the prospective client
- educate the buyer or seller about what a home is really worth
- analyze an investment property—whether it's a home with an extra apartment or an office complex
- determine closing costs
- calculate commissions

As you walk through *Real Estate Math*, you'll discover how to do all these and much more. Those of you who bought this book because you are studying for the exam will find problems similar to those you'll encounter on the test. Regardless of whether you are a student or on-the-job, this book provides the math skills you need. And it does so simply and clearly.

WHAT YOU'LL FIND IN *REAL ESTATE MATH*

Each step of the tour is clearly marked with:

- tips to remind you of a mathematical quirk or something to consider or remember
- clearly marked examples that guide you through the problem and show you how each part of the solution relates to what went before and what comes next
- "What You Need to Know," which provides quick conversions needed to solve some of the problems in that chapter
- an extensive real estate glossary that also explains mathematical terms

As all good walk-throughs do, *Real Estate Math* begins at the front door and allows you to assess where you are with a pretest covering many of the everyday problems professionals encounter. Not to worry: There's an answer key with explanations that guide you each step of the way through each problem! Like a fact sheet on a property for sale, the pretest will give you a feeling for the areas where you need to do a little work and the areas where you are strong. Chapter 1 provides a refresher that will help you to brush up those areas that need a little review (and gives you a handy reference just in case you need an occasional reminder).

Moving farther into *Real Estate Math*, Part 2 of the tour begins with the math you need to sell the property—all the way from qualifying the customer to the ins and outs of evaluating mortgages and estimating total monthly payments.

Moving right along, Part 3 takes you through all the math you need to know to evaluate both residential and investment properties and guide your clients—buyers and sellers—through their options.

Speaking of investment properties, Part 4 of the tour goes into the mathematical intricacies of evaluating investment property—large and small. Everything from income to appreciation and depreciation is examined. Last, but definitely not least, Part 5 walks you through closing costs and commissions.

How to Get the Most from This Book

We recommend that you begin the tour at the beginning and walk through at your own pace—you may be stronger in some areas than others—until you reach the end. Each chapter follows a logical progression and builds on the knowledge gained in previous chapters. In addition, each chapter contains fully worked-out, fully explained examples and practice problems that let you see how well you are doing as you move along. Like a well-designed house plan, this format allows you to go at your own pace, stopping wherever and whenever you want to polish your skills. You can even go back to the real estate math review in Chapter 1 if, for example, dividing fractions gives you a headache.

After you have walked through the entire book, take the posttest. It will tell you how far you have come, and if you find that you still need some polishing in some areas, return to those chapters and concentrate on them.

Caveat emptor: Financial calculators as well as tools on the Internet can be helpful, but in order to use them properly, you need to understand the basic mathematical principles that make them work. Otherwise, you could end up inputting the wrong data or dividing when you should be multiplying! What they say about computers applies to math as well: garbage in, garbage out. Once you understand the math, you'll be able to maximize the tools.

REAL ESTATE MATH

PART

ASSESSING YOUR SKILLS

PRETEST

This test will help you determine your strengths and weaknesses. Read each question carefully and then work the problem (use scratch paper for your calculations). The answers, which appear at the end of the chapter, show step by step how we arrived at each answer.

1. A borrower wants to know if he qualifies for a $400,000 conventional mortgage. His monthly income is $25,750, estimated PITI is $4,500, car payment is $400 per month, and child support is $2,000 per month. Does he qualify?

2. The purchase price of a house is $280,550. How large would the mortgage be if the down payment were 15%?

3. The purchase price of a home is $175,000. How much cash would the buyer need for the down payment if the first mortgage were 80% and the carryback were 10%?

4. Assuming that the appraised value and the selling price was $160,000 in a low-closing-cost state and that the closing costs are $325, calculate the total FHA mortgage.

5. How much is owed on a $512,000 loan after 5 months if the interest rate is 9.9%?

6. Find the rate of interest on a $64,000 loan, if the amount of interest paid after 2 years is $9,000.

7. A borrower is charged 4 points to get a 6.2% $322,000 mortgage. How much will the 4 points cost the borrower?

8. Assume you took out a $627,000 30-year mortgage 15 years ago. The interest rate is 8.5%, and your monthly payment is $4,821.09. If only 33% of your principal has been paid, how much interest has been paid?

9. A 25-year mortgage of $333,500 with an interest rate of 7.1% has monthly loan payments of $2,378.43. What is the loan constant?

10. If the purchase price of a home is $187,405 and the mortgage is $162,500, what is the LTV?

11. Assume that the borrower has purchased a property for $635,650 and has put 27.5% down. Calculate the transfer taxes, assuming the intangible tax rate is $.22 per $100 and the documentary stamp tax rate is $.305.

12. A home sold for $2.25 million. Determine the assessed taxable value if the rate of assessment is 19%.

13. Assume a cap rate of $2.25 for every $100 in assessed valuation. A property is assessed at $162,000, and the total property tax rate is $.088 per $100. How much tax is due on this property?

14. On a mortgage of $180,800, where the buyer is putting 15% down, the monthly mortgage payment at 7.3% is $1,312.66. Calculate the charge for PMI. Assuming no hazard insurance is required, what is the monthly payment?

15. How many acres are there in 612,000 square feet?

16. The replacement cost of a small, 25-year-old apartment building is $855,000; its estimated economic life is 75 years. What is the accrued depreciation using the straight-line method of depreciation?

17. Regarding the 25-year-old apartment building in question 16: Replacement cost is $855,000, its estimated economic life is 75 years, and its effective age is 17. What is the accrued depreciation?

18. The comparable property is on 16 acres and sold for $1.9 million. The estimated replacement value of the building is $1.55 million; the accrued depreciation is estimated at $325,000. The selling price for vacant land based on comparables is $33,000 per acre. The actual property is on a 22-acre lot. What is the value of the actual property's land?

19. Using the following table, calculate the +/– value of the comparable and subject homes and the estimated market value of the subject property.

Comparable Property	+/– Value	Subject Property	+/– Value
none		Bluestone patio	$7,500
Landscaped pool	$22,000	none	
Marble master bathroom, one year old	$25,000	none	

Comparable Property	+/– Value	Subject Property	+/– Value
Powder room ($\frac{1}{2}$ bath)	$2,500		
none		Finished walk-out basement with kitchen and bath	$100,000
		Landscaping in poor condition	($15,000)
Total +/–			
Selling price comparable	$575,000	**Selling price subject**	

20. The projected gross income of a building is $263,400; the property has a vacancy and collection rate of 12.75%. Calculate the gross operating income. The operating expense is $52,725.

21. What is the net operating income of the building in question 20?

22. Calculate the capitalization rate if the comparable sold for $239,500 and its NOI is $54,100.

23. On a property selling for $574,000, the gross income is $8,625 per month, and there is additional income of $375 per month. Calculate the monthly GRM and the annual GIM.

24. Assume an investor sold a property after 2 years for $450,000; the discount rate is 9.5%. How much would the investor have had to pay in present dollars to break even on the investment?

25. An office rents for $125.75 per square foot; increases are tied to an index that has gone from 1.85 to 2.15. It has 32,320 square feet. What is the monthly rent?

Use the following information to answer questions 26–32.

Assume an investment of $1,435,000 in a residential building with 10 apartments. There is an 80%, 30-year mortgage at 7.2% and monthly payments of $9,740.61. The building has 10 apartments: two studios that each rent for $1,600 per month, 4 one-bedroom apartments that rent for $3,000 per month, and 4 two-bedroom apartments that rent for $5,000 per month. Collection losses are 12.5% and estimated operating expenses are 40% of EGI.

26. What is the PGI?

27. What is the VCL?

28. What is the EGI?

29. What is the OE?

30. What is the NOI?

31. What is the yearly mortgage payment?

32. What is the PCTF?

33. An owner resides in 20% of an apartment building purchased for $750,675; the land is valued at $123,000. What is the owner's depreciable basis?

Use the following information to answer questions 34–38.

A residential building was purchased 5 years ago for $872,000. The land was evaluated at $174,400 at time of purchase. The property just sold for $1,044,000. Selling expenses are $75,200, and the balance owed on the mortgage is $697,600.

34. Calculate depreciation.

35. Calculate adjusted basis.

36. Calculate capital gains tax.

37. Calculate excess gain tax.

38. Calculate after-tax income.

Use the following information to answer questions 39–41.

A closing is on November 7; property taxes paid in arrears twice a year on July 1 (for January 1–June 30) and January 1 (for July 1–December 31) are $6,250 per year. The closing date is the buyer's responsibility.

39. Using the 365-day method, for how many days does the seller owe the buyer?

40. What is the average cost per day?

41. How much does the seller owe the buyer?

Use the following information to answer questions 42–44.

Using the 365-day method, assume annual taxes of $8,500, payment is made in quarterly installments on March 15 for the period of November 1 (of the preceding year)–January 31; June 15 for February 1–April 30; September 15 for May 1–July 31, and September 15 for August 1–October 31. Closing date is March 15, and the seller is responsible through March 14.

42. Using the 365-day method, for how many days does the seller owe the buyer?

43. What is the average cost per day?

44. How much does the seller owe the buyer?

45. A small office building has a rent roll of $57,150 per month, collected on the 1st. Closing is on August 11. The seller retains the income for day of closing. How much does the seller have to reimburse the buyer?

46. Water bills are averaging $313 per quarter and are paid in advance: January 1, April 1, July 1, and October 1. If closing is December 2, how much will the buyer need to reimburse the seller? The seller will pay for the day of closing. Use the 365-day method.

47. A seller wants to net $137,275 after commission. The mortgage balance is $287,000. The agent's commission is 6%. Assuming no other costs, what would the property have to sell for to achieve these goals?

48. Yearly taxes on an office building are $30,650. They are paid in arrears quarterly on the last day of each quarter. The closing date is March 3. This is a leap year. Using the 30-day method, how much does the seller owe the buyer if the seller is responsible for the closing date?

Use the following information to answer questions 49–52.

A home is listed at $339,500 and in a bidding war sells for $365,500. Calculate:

49. the total commission at 6%

50. the commission if split 50–50 between two brokerage agencies

51. the first sales associate's commission at 55%

52. the second sales associate's commission at 53.5%

ANSWERS

Answers appear in **boldface**.

1. **Yes, both ratios are below the 28% and 36% limits.**

   $4,500 (PITI) ÷ $25,750 (monthly income) = .17 or 17% housing expense ratio

   $4,500 (PITI) + ($400 + $2,000) ÷ $25,750 =

   $4,500 + $2,400 ÷ $25,750 =

   $6,900 ÷ $25,750 = **.267** or **27%** = total obligations ratio

2. $280,550 × .85 = **$238,467.5** mortgage

3. 80% + 10% = 90%

   $175,000 × 10% = **$17,500** cash

4. [$160,000 (selling price) + $325] × 97.15% (% available) =

   $160,325 × .9715 = $155,755.74 (maximum loan)

   $160,325 × .03 = $4,809.75 (minimum cash investment)

   $160,325 − $155,555.74 = $4,569.26

   $4,809.75 − $4,569.26 = $240.49

   $155,755.74 − $240.49 = $155,515.25 or **$155,515** (rounded to nearest dollar)

5. $I = P (\$512,000) \times R (9.9\%) \times \frac{1}{12}$ year

   $= \$512,000 \times 9.9\% \times \frac{1}{12}$

   $= \$512,000 \times .099 \times \frac{1}{12} = \$4,224$

   $4,224 × 5 = **$21,120**

6. $R = \frac{I (\$9,000)}{P (\$64,000) \times T (2\ \text{years})}$

   $= \frac{\$9,000}{\$64,000 \times 2}$

   $= \frac{\$9,000}{\$128,000}$

   $= \$9,000 ÷ \$128,000$

   $= **.070**$ or **7%** rate of interest

7. $322,000 × .04 = **$12,880**

8. Total paid – principal paid = interest paid

$4,821.09 (monthly payment) × 15 (years) × 12 (months) =

$867,796.20 (total paid to date)

$627,000 (total mortgage) × .33 = $206,910 (principal paid)

$867,796.20 – $206,910 = **$660,886.20** interest paid

9. $2,378.43 ÷ $333,500 = **.0071317** loan constant

10. $162,500 (mortgage) ÷ $187,405 (purchase price) = **.867** or **87%** LTV

11. $635,650 sales price × .725 financing = $460,846.25

$460,846.25 ÷ 100 = $4,608.4625 taxable hundreds

$4,608.46 × $.22 = **$1,013.86** intangible tax due

$4,608.46 × $.305 = **$1,405.58** (rounded) documentary stamp tax

12. $2,250,000 × .81 = **$1,822,500** taxable value

13. $162,000 (assessed value) ÷ 100 = 1,620 hundreds

$2.25 × 1,620 = $3,645

$162,000 × .032 = $5,184

$3,645 property tax owed

14. $180,800 (total mortgage) × .005 (annual PMI) = $\frac{\$904}{12}$ (monthly PMI)

$904 (PMI) ÷ 12 = $75.33 (monthly PMI)

$1,312.66 (monthly mortgage) + $75.33 = **$1,387.99** monthly payment

15. 612,000 square ÷ 43,560 square feet = **14.05** acres

16. $855,000 (replacement cost new) ÷ 75 (years of economic life) = $11,400 (depreciation per year)

$11,400 × 25 (age of structure) = **$285,000** accrued depreciation

17. [17 (effective age) ÷ 75 (economic life)] = .227 (age-life accrued depreciation) × $855,000 (replacement cost) = **$194,085** accrued depreciation

18. $1,550,000 (replacement cost) − $325,000 (accrued depreciation) = $1,225,000 (depreciated value of building)

$1,900,000 (selling price) − $1,225,000 (depreciated value of building) = $675,000

$675,000 (selling price of vacant land) ÷ 16 acres (size of comparable property) = $42,187.50 (value of land per acre)

$42,187.50 (price per acre) × 22 acres (size of actual property) = **$928,125** value of actual property's land

19. $575,000 (selling price per comparable) − ($22,000 + $25,000 + 2,500) + ($7,500 − $30,000 + $100,000 − $15,000) = 588,000

$588,000 − $49,500 + $62,500 = **$601,000** selling price subject

20. $263,400 (PGI) × 12.75% (VCL) = $33,583.50 (VCL in $)

$263,400 − $33,583.50 = **$229,816.50** GOI

21. $229,816.50 − $55,725 (OE) = **$174,091.50** NOI

22. $54,100 (NOI) ÷ $239,500 (selling price) = **.226** CAP rate

23. $574,000 (selling price) ÷ $8,625 (monthly rent + other income) = monthly GRM

$574,00 ÷ $9,000 = **66.55** monthly GRM

$574,000 ÷ ($9,000 × 12) (annual rent + annual other income) = annual GIM

$574,000 ÷ $108,000 = **5.3** annual GIM

24. $108,038.02

Year	Cash Flow	Discount	Discounted Value
1	$450,000	1.095	$410,958.90
2	$450,000	1.199	$108,038.02

25. 2.15 − 1.85 = .3

.3 ÷ 1.85 = .16 (rounded) or 16% increase

$125.75 × 1.16 = $145.87

$145.87 × 32,320 sq. ft. = **$4,714,518.4**

26. $2 \times \$1,600 + 4 \times 3,000 + 4 \times \$5,000$
($\$3,200 + \$12,000 + \$20,000) \times 12 =$
$\$35,200 \times 12 = \textbf{\$422,400}$ PGI

27. $\$422,400 \times .125 = \textbf{\$52,800}$ VCL

28. $\$422,400 - \$55,300 = \textbf{\$367,100}$ EGI

29. $\$367,100 \times .4 = \textbf{\$146,840}$ OE

30. $\$367,100 - \$146,840 = \textbf{\$220,260}$ NOI

31. $\$9,740.61 \times 12 = \textbf{\$116,887.32}$ yearly mortgage payment

32. $\$232,260 - \$116,887.32 = \textbf{\$115,372.68}$ BTCF

33. $\$750,675$ (purchase price) $- \$123,000 = \$627,675$
$\$627,675 \times 80\% = \$502,140$ depreciable basis
$\$502,140 \div 27.5 = \textbf{\$18,259.64}$

34. ($\$872,000$ [purchase price] $- \$174,400$ [value of land] = balance due on mortgage) $\div 27.5 =$ depreciable basis
($\$697,600 \div 27.5) \times 5$ (years) =
$\$25,367.27 \times 5 = \textbf{\$126,836.35}$ depreciation taken

35. $\$872,000$ (original purchase price) $- \$126,836.35$ (depreciation taken) =
$\textbf{\$745,163.65}$ adjusted basis

36. $\$1,044,000$ (selling price) $- \$745,163.65$ (adjusted basis) $- \$75,200$ (selling expense) $= \$223,636.40$ capital gain
$\$228,636.40 \times .15 = \textbf{\$33.545.46}$ capital gains tax

37. $\$223,636.40$ (capital gain) $- [\$1,044,000$ (selling price) $- \$872,000$ (purchase price)]
$\$223,636.40 - \$172,000 = \$51,636.40$ excess gain
$\$51,636.40 \times .25 = \textbf{\$12,909.10}$ excess gains tax

38. $\$1,044,000$ (selling price) $- \$697,600$ (mortgage balance) $- \$75,200$ (selling expenses) $- \$33,545.46 - \$12,909.10$ (taxes owed) $= \textbf{\$224,745.44}$ after-tax income

39. 31 (July) + 31 (August) + 30 (September) + 31 (October) + 6 (November) = **129** days

40. $6,250 ÷ 365 = **$17.123288** average cost per day

41. $17.123288 × 129 = **$2,208.90** (rounded)

42. 28 (February) + 14 (March) = **42** days

43. $8,500 ÷ 365 days = **$23.287671** average cost per day

44. $23.287671 × 42 = **$978.08** (rounded)

45. 31 − 11 = 20 days
($57,150 ÷ 31) = $1,843.5484 average cost per day
20 × $1,843.5484 = **$36,870.97**

46. $313 ÷ 92 = $3.40/day
$3.40 × 29 (days after December 2) = **$98.60**

47. 100% (total selling price) − 6% (total commission) = 94%
$287,000 (mortgage balance) + $137,275 (to seller) = $424,275
$424,275 ÷ .94 = **$451,356.38**

48. 31 (January) + 29 (February) + 3 (March) = 63 days
$30,650 ÷ 360 = $85.138888 cost per day
$85.138888 × 63 = **$5,363.75** (rounded)

49. $365,500 × .06 = **$21,930** total commission

50. $21,930 × .5 = **$10,965** commission if split 50–50

51. $10,965 × .55 = **$6,030.75** first sales associate's commission

52. $10,965 × .535 = **$5,866.28** (rounded) the second sales associate's commission

1

REAL ESTATE MATH REVIEW

CHAPTER SUMMARY

Whether you are a real estate professional or an investor in real estate, math is a vital tool, one you will need to call on frequently. Knowledge of real estate math will help increase your earnings, win you clients, and generally increase your bottom line. So, even if you weren't a whiz at math in school, this chapter will give you the foundation you'll need in your career.

Here are the types of math you will encounter in this chapter:

- percents
- areas
- property tax
- loan-to-value ratios
- points
- equity
- qualifying buyers
- prorations
- commissions

- sale proceeds
- transfer tax/conveyance tax/revenue stamps
- competitive market analyses (CMA)
- income properties
- depreciation

Keep in mind that although the math topics are varied, you will be using the same math skills to complete each question. But before you review your math skills, take a look at some helpful strategies for doing your best.

STRATEGIES FOR MATH QUESTIONS
Use Scratch Paper

Resist the temptation to "save time" by doing all your work on your calculator. The main pitfall with calculators is the temptation to work the problem all the way through to the end on the calculator.

Check Your Work

Checking your work is always good practice, and it's usually quite simple. Even if you come up with an answer that seems correct, you should check your work.

REAL ESTATE MATH REVIEW

Here's a quick review of some basic arithmetic, algebra, geometry, and word problem skills.

Arithmetic Review
Symbols of Multiplication

When two or more numbers are being multiplied, they are called **factors**. The answer that results is called the **product**.

> *Example:*
> $5 \times 6 = 30$ 5 and 6 are **factors** and 30 is the **product**.

There are several ways to represent multiplication in the above mathematical statement.

- A dot between factors indicates multiplication:

  $5 \cdot 6 = 30$

- Parentheses around one or more factors indicates multiplication:

  $(5)6 = 30, 5(6) = 30,$ and $(5)(6) = 30$

- Multiplication is also indicated when a number is placed next to a variable:

  $5a = 30$ In this equation, 5 is being multiplied by a.

Divisibility

Like multiplication, division can be represented in a few different ways:

$8 \div 3 \qquad 3\overline{)8} \qquad \frac{8}{3}$

In each of the above, 3 is the **divisor** and 8 is the **dividend**.

 ## How to Round

If the number after the one you need to round is 5 or more, make the preceding number one higher. If it is less than 5, drop it and leave the preceding number the same.

Example:
$0.0135 = .014$ or $.01$

Decimals

The most important thing to remember about decimals is that the first place value to the right begins with tenths. The place values are as follows:

1	2	6	8	•	3	4	5	7
THOUSANDS	HUNDREDS	TENS	ONES	DECIMAL POINT	TENTHS	HUNDREDTHS	THOUSANDTHS	TEN THOUSANDTHS

In expanded form, this number can also be expressed as . . .

$1,268.3457 = (1 \times 1,000) + (2 \times 100) + (6 \times 10) + (8 \times 1) + (3 \times .1) +$
$(4 \times .01) + (5 \times .001) + (7 \times .0001)$

Fractions

To do well when working with fractions, it is necessary to understand some basic concepts. Here are some math rules for fractions using variables:

$$\frac{a}{b} \times \frac{c}{d} = \frac{a \times c}{b \times d}$$

$$\frac{a}{b} + \frac{c}{b} = \frac{a+c}{b}$$

$$\frac{a}{b} \div \frac{c}{d} = \frac{a}{b} \times \frac{d}{c} = \frac{a \times d}{b \times c}$$

$$\frac{a}{b} + \frac{c}{d} = \frac{ad+bc}{bd}$$

Multiplication of Fractions

Multiplying fractions is one of the easiest operations to perform. To multiply fractions, simply multiply the numerators and the denominators, writing each in the respective place over or under the fraction bar.

Example:

$$\frac{4}{5} \times \frac{6}{7} = \frac{24}{35}$$

Dividing of Fractions

Dividing fractions is the same thing as multiplying fractions by their **reciprocals**. To find the reciprocal of any number, switch its numerator and denominator. For example, the reciprocals of the following numbers are:

$$\frac{1}{3} \rightarrow \frac{3}{1} = 3$$

$$x \rightarrow \frac{1}{x}$$

$$\frac{4}{5} \rightarrow \frac{5}{4}$$

$$5 \rightarrow \frac{1}{5}$$

When dividing fractions, simply multiply the dividend (the number being divided) by the divisor's (the number doing the dividing) reciprocal to get the answer.

Example:

$$\frac{12}{21} \div \frac{3}{4} = \frac{12}{21} \times \frac{4}{3} = \frac{48}{63} = \frac{16}{21}$$

Adding and Subtracting Fractions

To add or subtract fractions with the same denominator, just add or subtract the numerators and leave the denominator as it is. For example,

$$\frac{1}{7} + \frac{5}{7} = \frac{6}{7} \text{ and } \frac{5}{8} - \frac{2}{8} = \frac{3}{8}$$

Sometimes the result may be larger than 1. When this happens, you should reduce the fraction to its lowest form. This means you must find its **greatest common denominator** (GCD), the *largest* number that can be divided evenly into both numbers. For example,

$$\frac{7}{8} + \frac{5}{8} = \frac{12}{8}$$

Thus, 4 is the GCD because $12 \div 4 = 3$ and $8 \div 4 = 2$. In other words, the GCD is the *largest* common factor that can be divided into each of the denominators.

Doing that, you get $\frac{3}{2}$, which is an improper fraction.

Therefore, you must take the process a step further, and convert the fraction into a mixed numeral; to do this, you divide 3 by 2 to get $1\frac{1}{2}$.

To add or subtract fractions with different denominators, you must find the **lowest common denominator** (LCD)—that is, the number that both denominators can be divided into evenly.

For example, if the denominators are 8 and 12, then 24 is the LCD because $8 \times 3 = 24$ and $12 \times 2 = 24$. In other words, the LCD is the *smallest* multiple divisible by each of the denominators.

Once you know the LCD, convert each fraction by multiplying both the numerator and denominator by the necessary factor to get the LCD, and then add or subtract the new numerators.

Example:

$$\frac{1}{3} + \frac{2}{5} = \frac{5(1)}{5(3)} + \frac{3(2)}{3(5)} = \frac{5}{15} + \frac{6}{15} = \frac{11}{15}$$

Percent

A **percent** is a measure of a part to a whole, with the whole being equal to 100.

- To change a decimal to a percentage, move the decimal point two units to the right and add a percentage symbol.

  Example:

  .45 = 45%   .07 = 7%   .9 = 90%

- To change a fraction to a percentage, first change the fraction to a decimal. To do this, divide the numerator by the denominator. Then, change the decimal to a percentage.

  Example:

  $\frac{4}{5} = .80 = 80\%$

  $\frac{2}{5} = .4 = 40\%$

  $\frac{1}{8} = .125 = 12.5\%$

- To change a percentage to a decimal, simply move the decimal point two places to the left and eliminate the percentage symbol.

  Example:

  64% = .64   87% = .87   7% = .07

- To change a percentage to a fraction, divide by 100 and reduce.

  Example:

  $64\% = \frac{64}{100} = \frac{16}{25}$

  $75\% = \frac{75}{100} = \frac{3}{4}$

  $82\% = \frac{82}{100} = \frac{41}{50}$

- Keep in mind that any percentage that is 100 or greater will need to reflect a whole number or mixed number when converted.

  Example:

  $125\% = 1.25$ or $1\frac{1}{4}$

  $350\% = 3.5$ or $3\frac{1}{2}$

Here are some conversions you should be familiar with:

Fraction	Decimal	Percentage
$\frac{1}{2}$	.5	50%
$\frac{1}{4}$	.25	25%
$\frac{1}{3}$	.333 . . .	33.$\overline{3}$%
$\frac{2}{3}$	.666 . . .	66.$\overline{6}$%
$\frac{1}{10}$	.1	10%
$\frac{1}{8}$	.125	12.5%
$\frac{1}{6}$	.1666 . . .	16.$\overline{6}$%
$\frac{1}{5}$	.2	20%

Algebra Review

Equations

An **equation** is solved by finding a number that is equal to an unknown variable.

Simple Rules for Working with Equations

1. The equal sign separates an equation into two sides.
2. Whenever an operation is performed on one side, the same operation must be performed on the other side.
3. Your first goal is to get all of the variables on one side and all of the numbers on the other.
4. The final step often will be to divide each side by the coefficient, leaving the variable equal to a number.

Solving Equations

To solve the equation $\frac{x}{6} = \frac{x+10}{12}$, eliminate the denominators by multiplying the numerators and the denominators:

$$12x = 6x + 60$$

Subtract $6x$ from both sides of the equation:

$$6x = 60$$
$$x = 10$$

Checking Equations

To check an equation, substitute the number equal to the variable in the original equation.

> ### Example:
>
> To check the equation below, substitute the number 10 for the variable x.
>
> $$\frac{x}{6} = \frac{x+10}{12}$$
>
> $$\frac{10}{6} = \frac{10+10}{12}$$
>
> $$\frac{10}{6} = \frac{20}{12}$$
>
> $$1\frac{2}{3} = 1\frac{2}{3} \quad \frac{10}{6} = \frac{10}{6}$$
>
> Because this statement is true, you know the answer $x = 10$ must be correct.

Algebraic Fractions

Algebraic fractions are very similar to fractions in arithmetic.

> ### Example:
>
> Write $\frac{x}{5} - \frac{x}{10}$ as a single fraction.
>
> ### Solution:
>
> Just like in arithmetic, you need to find the LCD of 5 and 10, which is 10. Then change each fraction into an equivalent fraction that has 10 as a denominator.
>
> $$\frac{x}{5} - \frac{x}{10} = \frac{x(2)}{5(2)} - \frac{x}{10}$$
>
> $$= \frac{2x}{10} - \frac{x}{10}$$
>
> $$= \frac{x}{10}$$

Geometry Review

Area	the space inside a two-dimensional figure
Circumference	the distance around a circle
Perimeter	the distance around a figure
Radius	the distance from the center point of a circle to any point on the outside of the circle

Area

Area is the space inside of the lines defining the shape.

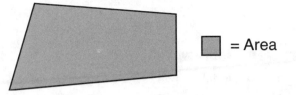

This geometry review will focus on the area formula for three main shapes: circles, rectangles/squares, and triangles.

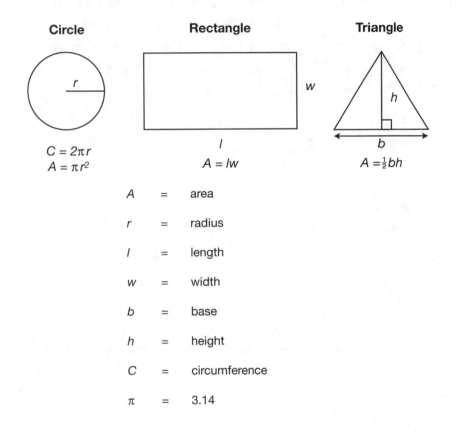

Circle	Rectangle	Triangle
$C = 2\pi r$		
$A = \pi r^2$	$A = lw$	$A = \frac{1}{2}bh$

$$A \quad = \quad \text{area}$$

$$r \quad = \quad \text{radius}$$

$$l \quad = \quad \text{length}$$

$$w \quad = \quad \text{width}$$

$$b \quad = \quad \text{base}$$

$$h \quad = \quad \text{height}$$

$$C \quad = \quad \text{circumference}$$

$$\pi \quad = \quad 3.14$$

Perimeter

The perimeter of an object is simply the sum of all of its sides.

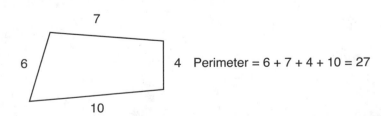

Perimeter = 6 + 7 + 4 + 10 = 27

The circumference is the perimeter of a circle.

$C = 2\pi r$

Word Problem Review

If you are preparing to take a real estate exam, many of the math problems will be word problems, so pay extra attention to the following review.

Translating Words into Numbers

The most important skill needed for word problems is being able to translate words into mathematical operations. The following will assist you by giving you some common examples of English phrases and their mathematical equivalents.

- "Increase" means add.

  Example:
  A number increased by five = $x + 5$.

- "Less than" means subtract.

  Example:
  10 less than a number = $x - 10$.

- "Times" or "product" means multiply.

  Example:
  Three times a number = $3x$.

- "Times the sum" means to multiply a number by a quantity in parentheses.

  Example:
  Five times the sum of a number and three = $5(x + 3)$.

- Two variables are sometimes used together.

  Example:
  A number y exceeds five times a number x by ten = $y = 5x + 10$.

- "Of" means multiply.

  Example:
  10% of 100 is 10 = $10\% \times 100 = 10$.

- "Is" means equals.

Example:

15 is 14 plus 1 becomes $15 = 14 + 1$.

Assigning Variables in Word Problems

Sometimes you will need to create and assign variables in a word problem. To do this, first identify an unknown and a known. You may not actually know the exact value of the "known," but you will know at least something about its value.

Mr. Maxwell's house is three years older than Ms. Richards's house.
Unknown = age of Ms. Richards's house = x
Known = Mr. Maxwell's house is 3 years older.
Therefore, the age of Ms. Richard's house = $x + 3$

Heidi sold twice as many houses as John.
Unknown = number of houses John sold = x
Known = number of houses Heidi sold = $2x$

The Main Street apartment building has five more than three times the number of apartments than the Elm Street apartment building has.

Known = the number of apartments in the Elm Street building = x
Unknown = the number of apartments in the Main Street building
= $3x + 5$

Percentage Problems

There is one formula that is useful for solving the three types of percentage problems:

$$\frac{\text{part}}{\text{whole}} = \frac{\%}{100}$$

or

$$\frac{\text{"is"}}{\text{"of"}} = \frac{\%}{100}$$

When reading a percentage problem, substitute the necessary information into the above formula based on the following:

- 100 is always written in the denominator of the percentage sign column.
- If given a percentage, write it in the numerator position of the number column. If you are not given a percentage, then the variable should be placed there.
- The denominator of the number column represents the number that is equal to the whole, or 100%. This number always follows the word *of* in a word problem.
- The numerator of the number column represents the number that is the percent.
- In the formula, the equal sign can be interchanged with the word *is*.

Examples:

- Finding a percentage of a given number:
  What number is equal to 40% of 50?

$$\frac{\overset{\#}{x}}{50} = \frac{\overset{\%}{40}}{100}$$

Cross multiply:

$100(x) = (40)(50)$

$100x = 2{,}000$

$\frac{100x}{100} = \frac{2{,}000}{100}$

$x = 20$ Therefore, 20 is 40% of 50.

▶ How Are Rate Problems Defined?

$$\text{Rate} = \frac{x \text{ units}}{y \text{ units}}$$

A percentage problem simply means that *y* units is equal to 100. It is important to remember that a percentage problem may be worded using the word *rate*.

- Finding a number when a percentage is given:
  40% of what number is 24?

$$\frac{\overset{\#}{24}}{x} = \frac{\overset{\%}{40}}{100}$$

Cross multiply:

$(24)(100) = (40)(x)$

$2,400 = 40x$

$\frac{2,400}{40} = \frac{40x}{40}$

$60 = x$ Therefore, 40% of 60 is 24.

- Finding what percentage one number is of another:

  What percentage of 75 is 15?

$$\frac{\overset{\#}{15}}{75} = \frac{\overset{\%}{x}}{100}$$

Cross multiply:

$15(100) = (75)(x)$

$1,500 = 75x$

$\frac{1,500}{75} = \frac{75x}{75}$

$20 = x$ Therefore, 20% of 75 is 15.

Rate Problems

You may encounter a couple of different types of rate problems: cost per unit, interest rate, and tax rate. **Rate** is defined as a comparison of two quantities with different units of measure.

$\text{Rate} = \frac{x \, \text{units}}{y \, \text{units}}$

Examples: $\frac{\text{dollars}}{\text{square foot}}, \frac{\text{interest}}{\text{year}}$

Cost Per Unit

Some problems may require that you calculate the cost per unit.

Example:

If 100 square feet cost $1,000, how much does 1 square foot cost?

Solution:

$= \frac{1,000}{100} = \$10$ per square foot

Interest Rate

The formula for simple interest is Interest = Principal × Rate × Time or $I = PRT$. If you know certain values, but not others, you can still find the answer using algebra. In simple interest problems, the value of T is usually 1, as in 1 year. There are three basic kinds of interest problems, depending on which number is missing.

Equivalencies

Here are some equivalencies you may need to use to complete some questions.

> *Equivalencies*
> 12 inches (in. or ") = 1 foot (ft. or ')
> 3 feet or 36 inches = 1 yard (yd.)
> 1,760 yards = 1 mile (mi.)
> 5,280 feet = 1 mile
> 144 square inches (sq. in. or in.^{2}) = 1 square foot (sq. ft. or ft.^{2})
> 9 square feet = 1 square yard
> 43,560 feet = 1 acre
> 640 acres = 1 square mile

Percents

It is helpful to know how to solve a basic percentage problem.

> *Example:*
> What is 86% of 1,750?

> *Solution:*
> Start by translating words into math terms.
> $x = (86\%)(1,750)$
> Change the percent into a decimal by moving the decimal point two spaces to the left.
> $86\% = .86$
> Now you can solve.
> $x = (.86)(1,750)$
> $x = 1,505$

Other percentage problems may come in the form of rate problems. Keep reading for more examples of these problems.

Interest Problems

Let's take a look at a problem in which you have to calculate the interest rate (R). Remember, the rate is the same as the percentage.

> *Example:*
> Mary Valencia borrowed $5,000, for which she is paying $600 interest per year. What is the rate of interest being charged?

> *Solution:*
> Start with the values you know.
> Principal = $5,000
> Interest = $600
> Rate = x
> Time = 1 year
> Using the formula $I = PRT$, insert the values you know, and solve for x.
> $600 = 5,000(x)(1)$
> $600 = 5,000x$
> $\frac{600}{5,000} = \frac{x}{5,000}$
> $.12 = x$
> To convert .12 to a percent, move the decimal point two places to the right.
> $.12 = 12\%$

Area

Some problems may ask you to calculate the area of a piece of land, a building, or some other figure. Here are some formulas and how to use them.

Rectangles

Remember the formula: Area = (length)(width).

> *Example:*
> A man purchased a lot that is 50 feet by 10 feet for a garden. How many square feet of land does he have?

> *Solution:*
> Using the formula, Area = (length)(width), you have:
> A = (50)(10) = 500 square feet

> *Example:*
> The Meyers family bought a piece of land for a summer home that was 2.75 acres. The lake frontage was 150 feet. What was the length of the lot?

Solution:

You will need to refer to the "Equivalencies" list on page 28 to answer this question. First, find the area of the land in square feet.

$(2.75)(43{,}560) = 119{,}790$ square feet

In the previous example, you were given the length and the width. In this example, you are given the area and the width, so you are solving for the length. Because you know the area and the width of the lot, use the formula to solve.

Area = (length)(width)

$119{,}790 = (x)(150)$

Divide both sides by 150.

$\frac{119{,}790}{150} = \frac{(x)(150)}{150}$

$x = \frac{119{,}790}{150}$

$x = 798.6$ feet

Triangles

Although it may not be as common, you may be asked to find the area of a triangle. If you don't remember the formula, see page 23.

Example:

The Baron family is buying a triangular piece of land for a gas station. It is 200 feet at the base, and the side perpendicular to the base is 200 feet. They are paying $2.00 per square foot for the property. What will it cost?

Solution:

Start with the formula Area = $\frac{1}{2}$(base)(height).

Now, write down the values you know.

Area = x

Base = 200

Height = 200

If it's easier, you can change $\frac{1}{2}$ to a decimal.

$\frac{1}{2} = .5$

Now you can plug these values into the formula.

$x = (.5)(200)(200)$

$x = (.5)(40{,}000)$

$x = 20{,}000$ square feet

Don't forget that the question is not asking for the number of square feet, but for the *cost* of the property per square foot. This is a rate problem, so you need to complete one more step: (20,000 square feet)($2 per square foot) = $40,000.

Example:

Victor and Evelyn Robinson have an outlot that a neighbor wants to buy. The side of the outlot next to their property is 86 feet. The rear line is perpendicular to their side lot, and the road frontage is 111 feet. Their plat shows they own 3,000 square feet in the outlot. What is the length of the rear line of the outlot? Round your answer to the nearest whole number.

Solution:

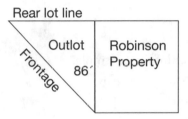

It helps to draw the figure to conceive shapes. The rear lot line is perpendicular to the side lot line. This makes the side lot line the base and the rear lot line the height (altitude).

Area = $\frac{1}{2}$(base)(height)

Area = 3,000 square feet

Base = 86 feet

Height = x

If it's easier, you can change $\frac{1}{2}$ to a decimal.

$\frac{1}{2}$ = .5

Now you can plug these values into the formula.

3,000 = (.5)(86)(x)

3,000 = (43)(x)

Divide both sides by 43.

$\frac{3,000}{43} = \frac{(43)(x)}{43}$

x = 69.767 feet

Don't forget the question says to round your answer to the nearest whole number. The answer is 70 feet.

Circles

Remember the formula Area $= \pi r^2$.

Example:

Murray Brodman, a contractor, has been awarded the job to put up a circular bandstand in the town square. The radius of the circular area for the bandstand is 15 feet. What is the area of the bandstand? Use 3.14 for π.

Solution:

Area $= \pi r^2$

Start with the values you know.

Area $= x$

$\pi = 3.14$

radius $= 15$

Now plug these values into the formula.

Area $= (3.14)(15)(15) = 706.5$ sq. ft.

PROPERTY TAX

To solve property tax questions, you will be using percents and rates.

Example:

The tax rate in your county is $4.17 per hundred of assessed valuation, and Mr. Brown, a possible client, has told you his taxes are $1,100. What is his property assessment? (Round your answer to the nearest 10 cents.)

Solution:

Start off with the values you know.

Taxes $= \$1,100$

Assessment $= x$

Tax rate $= \$4.17$ per hundred (%)

If you remember the definition of percent as being an amount per hundred, then $4.17 per hundred is actually 4.17%. To make this equation more manageable, convert this percent to a decimal by moving the decimal point two spaces to the left. Now the tax rate is .0417.

.0417 of the assessed value of the house is $1,100. Translate the words into math terms. This means:

$(.0417)(x) = 1,100.$

To solve the equation, divide both sides by .0417.

$$\frac{.0417x}{.0417} = \frac{1,100}{.0417}$$

$x = \$26,378.896$

Remember, the question asks you round to the nearest 10 cents.
That means that .896 needs to be rounded up to 90. So the answer is
$26,378.90.

Example:

Mr. Smith knew his own taxes were $975 and his property assess-
ment was $17,000 for the house and $6,000 for the land. He wanted
to know the tax rate (%).

Solution:

Start with the values you know.

Tax = $975

Assessment for house = $17,000, plus assessment for land = $6,000.

Therefore, total = $23,000.

Rate (%) = x

According to the question, $23,000 at a rate of x is $975. Convert this
statement into an equation.

($23,000)($x$) = 975.

Solve the equation by dividing both sides by 23,000.

$$\frac{23,000x}{23,000} = \frac{975}{23,000}$$

$x = .0423913$

To make this equation more simple, round the answer to .0424.
Remember that you are looking for the rate. Therefore, you need to
convert this decimal to a percent by moving the decimal point two
places to the right. The rate is 4.24%. (This can also be expressed as
$4.24 per hundred.)

▶ *Tip*

Note that you may be asked for monthly amounts in certain problems. Most
calculations are on an annual basis—unless you divide by 12.

Loan-to-Value Ratios

These problems often deal with percentages.

Example:

A mortgage loan for 10% is at a 75% loan-to-value ratio. The interest on the original balance for the first year is $6,590. What is the value of the property securing the loan? Round to the nearest one cent.

Solution:

First, find out the loan amount.

$6,590 is 10% of the loan amount. Let x equal the loan amount.

Now, translate these words into math terms.

$6,590 = (10\%)(x)$

Change 10% into a decimal by moving the decimal point two places to the left.

$10\% = .1$

Now you have:

$6,590 = (.1)(x)$

Divide both sides by (.1).

$x = \$65,900$

Now that you know the loan amount ($65,900), use this information to find the value of the property.

Write down the values you know.

Loan amount = $65,900

Loan-to-value ratio = 75%

Value = x

We know that 75% of the value is $65,900.

Translate this into math terms.

$(75\%)(x) = \$65,900$

Change the percent into a decimal (75% = .75) and solve.

$(.75)(x) = 65,900$

Divide both sides by .75.

$$\frac{(.75)(x)}{(.75)} = \frac{65,900}{(.75)}$$

$x = 87,866.66667$

When rounded to the nearest one cent, the answer is $87,866.67.

Points

Loan discounts are often called **points**, or loan placement fees, one point meaning 1% of the face amount of the loan. The service fee of 1% paid by buyers of government backed loans is called a **loan origination fee**.

Example:

A homebuyer may obtain a $50,000 FHA mortgage loan, provided the seller pays a discount of five points. What is the amount of the discount?

Solution:

The definition of one point is 1% of the face amount of the loan. Therefore, 5 points = 5% of the face of the loan. First, change the percent to a decimal.

5% = .05

Now you can use these values to solve.

Amount of discount = x

Points = .05

Amount of loan = $50,000

So, $x = (.05)(50,000)$.

$x = $2,500$

Example:

A property is listed at $74,000. An offer is made for $72,000, provided the seller pays three points on a loan for 80% of the purchase price. The brokerage commission rate is 7%. How much less will the seller receive if he accepts the offer than he would have received if he sold at all cash at the original terms?

Solution:

Here are the values you know:

Sold for original terms—price	$74,000	
Less 7% commission	− 5,180	(.07)(74,000) = 5,180
Seller's net	$68,820	

This question becomes more difficult, because in order to find the seller's net on the offered price, you must calculate the discount. The provision is that the seller pays 3 points (or .03) on a loan for 80% (or .8) of the price.

Start by finding 80% of the price.

$(.8)(72,000) = $57,600$

Now, the points are applied to this amount. This means .03 of $57,600 is the discount.

So, (.03)(57,600) = discount = 1,728.

You know these values:

Sold at offered terms—price	$72,000
Less 7% commission	− 5,040 (.07)(72,000) = 5,040
Less discount	− 1,728
Seller's net	$65,232

$72,000	Sales price		Net at original	$68,820
× .80	Loan-to-value ratio		Net at offered	−65,232
$57,600	Loan amount		Difference	$3,588
× .03	Points			
$1,728	Discount			

Equity

Example:

If a homeowner has a first mortgage loan balance of $48,350, a second mortgage loan balance of $18,200, and $26,300 equity, what is the value of her home?

Solution:

In this case, the value of the home is determined by the total loan balance plus the equity. Add the three numbers to find the value of the home.

$48,350 loan balance + $18,200 loan balance + $26,300 = value of the home

$92,850 = value of the home

Qualifying Buyers

Example:

A buyer is obtaining a conventional loan that requires $\frac{29}{33}$ ratios. He earns $66,000 a year and has a $1,350 car payment. What is his maximum PITI payment?

a. $1,692.50

b. $1,812.50

c. $1,595.00

d. $2,475.00

Solution:

$66,000 divided by 12 = $5,500 monthly income

$1,350 divided by 12 = monthly debt

($5,500)(.29) = $1,595 front-end qualifier

($5,500)(.33) = $1,815 – $112.50 debt = $1,692.50 back-end qualifier

Maximum PITI (Principal, Interest, Taxes, and Insurance) is the lower of these two qualifiers, $1,595.

Prorations

At the time of settlement, there must be a reconciliation or adjustment of any monies owed by either party as of that date. The important fact to bear in mind is that *the party who used the service pays for it.* If you will keep this firmly in mind you will not have any difficulty deciding who to credit and who to debit.

Example:

Mr. Seller's taxes are $1,200 a year paid in advance on a calendar year. He is settling on the sale of his house to Mr. Buyer on August 1. Which of them owes how much to the other?

Solution:

Ask yourself some questions:

How many months has the seller paid for?	12
($1,200)	
How many months has the seller used?	7
($700)	
How many months should the seller be reimbursed for?	5
($500)	
How many months will the buyer use?	5
($500)	
How many months has he paid for?	0
($0)	
How many months should he reimburse the seller for?	5
($500)	

Credit Mr. Seller $500

Debit Mr. Buyer $500

What would the answer be if the taxes were paid in arrears? In other words, the seller has used the service for seven months but hasn't paid anything. The buyer will have to pay it all at the end of the year. In that case, the seller owes the buyer for seven months, or $700.

▶ *Tip*

In working proration problems, be sure you have the right dates when you subtract. Sometimes, the termination date for the policy is not given, and the tendency is to subtract the date the policy was written from the date of settlement. This will not give you the unused portion. You must subtract the date of settlement from the date of termination of the policy, which will be exactly the same date, one, three, or five years after written, depending on the term of the policy. Most problems use either a one- or three-year term.

Remember!

Use a 30-day month and a 360-day year in all calculations unless you are told otherwise. Assume a calendar year, unless a fiscal or school year is specified.

Commissions

Let's look at a commission problem. They are typically rate (percentage) problems.

Example:

Broker Jones sold the Smith house for $65,000. The total commission came to $4,000. What was Jones's commission rate? Round to the nearest whole percent.

Solution:

You see the word *rate* and decide this is solved using percentages.
Start with the values you know.
Price of house = 65,000
Commission rate = x
Commission = 4,000

Now, translate the word problem into an equation.
$65,000x = 4,000$

Divide both sides by 65,000.
$x = \frac{4,000}{65,000}$
$x = 0.061$
Convert the decimal to a percent by moving the decimal two places to the right. 0.061 becomes 6.1%.

Example:

An agent received a 3% commission on $\frac{1}{4}$ of her total sales. On the remainder, she received a 6% commission. What was her average commission for all of her sales?

Solution:

Start off by asking yourself: How many fourths (parts) were there? Four, naturally.

3%   6%   6%   6%

To find the average, you add up all the numbers, and divide by the number of items you add together. In this case, there are four numbers.

So, 3 + 6 + 6 + 6 = 21.

And 21% ÷ 4 = 5.25%.

Sale Proceeds

Example:

Salesman Garcia was trying to list a house. The owner said he wanted to clear (net) $12,000 from the sale of the house. The balance of the mortgage was $37,000. It would cost about $1,200 to fix up the house to sell. How much would the owner have to sell the house for if the 7% commission was included? (Round your answer to the nearest cent.)

Solution:

Use a chart to clarify the problem.

Expenses	In Dollars	In Percents
Seller's net	12,000	
Loan balance	37,000	
Repairs	1,200	
Commission		7%
	50,200	7%

If the sales price is 100% and the commission is 7% of the sales price, all the remaining items added together must make 93% of the sales price. The place where most people go wrong is in not including the seller's net when they add the expenses. The seller's net has to come out of the sales price. (Where else would it come from?) Therefore, it is part of the remaining 93%. You now have a percentage problem. As always, convert your percents to decimals.

Start with the values you know:

Expenses = $50,200

Sales price = x

Seller's net, loan balance, repairs = .93 of sales price

.93 of the sales price is $50,200.

Convert this statement into an equation.

$(.93)(x) = \$50,200$

Divide both sides by .93.

$$\frac{(.93)(x)}{.93} = \frac{\$50,200}{.93}$$

$$x = \frac{\$50,200}{.93}$$

$x = \$53,978.4946$

Don't forget to round to the nearest cent!

$x = \$53,978.49$

Transfer Tax/Conveyance Tax/Revenue Stamps

Here is a transfer tax question.

Example:

A property is sold for $135,800 in cash. The transfer tax is $441.35. If transfer taxes are calculated per $200 of value, what was the rate (per $200) of the transfer tax?

Solution:

Start with the values you know.

Selling price = $135,800

Transfer tax rate = x per $200

Transfer tax = $441.35

It's probably easiest to begin by dividing by $200 since the rate is calculated per $200 of value.

So, $\frac{\$135,800}{\$200} = 679$ two hundreds

You know that $441.35 is produced by multiplying 679 by some rate.

Translate this into math terms.

$441.35 = (x)(679)$

Divide both sides by 679 to get

$$\frac{\$441.35}{(679)} = \frac{(x)(679)}{(679)}$$

$.65 = x$

Therefore, the transfer tax rate is $.65 per $200.

Competitive Market Analyses (CMA)

To solve these problems, you will use measurements and other hypothetical features of the comparable property to arrive at a value. Remember, a CMA is not an appraisal.

Example:

If Building A measures 52' by 106' and Building B measures 75' by 85', how much will B cost if A costs $140,000 and both cost the same per square foot to build?

Solution:

Area = (length)(width)

Area of Building A = (52)(106) = 5,512 square feet

Area of Building B = (75)(85) = 6,375 square feet

Cost of Building A per square foot = $\frac{140,000}{5,512}$ = $25.40

Cost of Building B = (6,375)($25.40) = $161,925

Example:

Carson's house (B), which is being appraised, is an exact twin of the houses on either side of it, built by the same builder at the same time. House A was appraised for $45,000, but it has a 14×20 foot garage which was added at a cost of about $18 per square foot. House C was recently sold for $43,000, with central air valued at $3,000. What would be a fair estimate of the value of Carson's house?

Solution:

Comparable C	$43,000
– Air Conditioning	−3,000
	$40,000

Comparable A $45,000   Garage: $14' \times 20' = 280$ sq. ft.

– Cost of Garage   – 5,040   280 sq. ft. $\times$ $18 = $5,040

                   $39,960

Answer: $40,000

Income Properties

Example:

An investor is considering the purchase of an income property generating a gross income of $350,000. Operating expenses constitute 70% of gross income. If the investor wants a return of 14%, what is the maximum he can pay?

Solution:

Gross income = $350,000

Expenses = 70% of gross income

Net income = Gross income – Expenses

Desired return = 14%

Maximum buyer can pay = x

This is a multi-step problem. Start by calculating the expenses, but remember you will need to stop to calculate the net income. First, change the percent to a decimal.

70% = .70

Now, you know that expenses are 70% of the gross income of $350,000. Change the words to mathematical terms.

Expenses = $(.7)(350,000) = $245,000

Gross income – Expenses = Net income

$350,000 – $245,000 = $105,000

The buyer wants the net income ($105,000) to be 14% of what he pays for the property.

Change the percent to a decimal (14% = .14) and then convert this statement to an equation.

$105,000 = (.14)(x)$

Divide both sides by .14.

$$\frac{\$105,000}{.14} = \frac{(.14)(x)}{.14}$$

$105,000 \div .14 = x$

$750,000 = x$

Depreciation

There are several methods of depreciation, and one you should know is the straight-line method. This method spreads the total depreciation over the useful life of the building in equal annual amounts. It is calculated by dividing the replacement cost by the years of useful life left.

$$\frac{\text{replacement cost}}{\text{years of useful life}} = \text{annual depreciation}$$

The depreciation rate may be given or may have to be calculated by the straight-line method. This means dividing the total depreciation (100%) by the estimated useful life given for the building.

$$\frac{100\%}{\text{years of useful life}} = \text{depreciated rate}$$

If a building has 50 years of useful life left, the depreciation rate would be computed as follows:

$$\frac{100\%}{50} = 2\%$$

In other words, it has a 2% depreciation rate annually.

Example:

The replacement cost of a building has been estimated at $80,000. The building is 12 years old and has an estimated 40 years of useful life left. What can be charged to annual depreciation? What is the total depreciation for 12 years? What is the present value of this building?

Solution:

Calculate the annual depreciation.

$\frac{\text{replacement cost}}{\text{years of useful life}} = \text{annual depreciation}$

$\frac{\$80,000}{40} = \$2,000$

Find the total depreciation over the 12 years.

Annual depreciation of $2,000 \times 12$ years $= \$24,000$.

Find the current value: replacement − depreciation = current value.

$\$80,000 - \$24,000 = \$56,000$

BEGIN YOUR MATH WALK-THROUGH

We hope that this review has helped you identify your strengths as well as any weaknesses you may have. No matter how well you did, we urge you to take this tour from the beginning, because each chapter builds on the skills that precede it. How long you spend on each section will depend on your own needs. Everyone can benefit from an occasional refresher.

SELLING REAL ESTATE

2

CALCULATING AFFORDABILITY AND EVALUATING MORTGAGES

PREQUALIFYING THE CUSTOMER

As every salesperson and broker knows, there is little point in spending time with a customer who can't afford to buy, so prequalifying the buyer is time well spent because it will help you determine:

- the types of financing available to the client
- the amount of financing available to the client
- the range of prices of property you should be showing the client

It is also a great way to educate prospective buyers who may be overestimating or underestimating what they can afford. And, most important, it will help you and your client find a lender. When a lender has formally preapproved your client, it may make or break a sale in a hot market.

Calculating the Size of the Mortgage

To prequalify a customer, you will need to know how to explain and how to calculate:

- gross income
- gross expenses
- percentage of gross income available for real estate taxes and homeowners insurance
- percentage of gross income available for mortgage principal and interest payments
- amount available for down payment

▶ *Before You Begin, You Need to Know . . .*

PITI = principal, interest, taxes, insurance
PITIO = principal, interest, taxes, insurance, and other long-term monthly nonhousing costs

Income

Calculating gross income requires simple math; making certain that all income is included in those calculations is more difficult. If more than one person is purchasing the property, ensure that you are calculating both incomes, including:

- income from *all* employment
- self-employment income
- dividends and interest that are *not* reinvested
- pension, 401(k), IRA, etc.
- rental income
- child support/alimony
- miscellaneous income

Income Example:
Assume both members of a couple are employed; he earns $115,000 per year, and she earns $75,000 per year. Together they receive interest and dividend income of $1,250, and she receives child support of $200 per week for two children from a previous marriage. The formula for calculating their total income is

$115,000 + $75,000 + $1,250 + ($200 × 52) =
$115,000 + $75,000 + $1,250 + $10,400 = $201,650
$201,650 ÷ 12 = $16,804.17 = total monthly income

Expenses

The second part is to determine their regular monthly expenses, *not* including their housing expenses or property taxes they pay. This takes a bit more work because people often don't know how they spend their money.

 Tip

Add 5% of the total for miscellaneous expenses.

Expense Example:

Let's stay with the couple in our income example and assume their monthly expenses are:

telephone, Internet, and cable TV	$ 175
medical payments	$ 200
utilities	$ 200
vacations	$ 250
retirement fund contributions	$1,092
insurance	$ 750
public transportation	$ 150
groceries	$1,200
dues and memberships	$ 165
student loans	$1,000
clothing	$ 75
car payments (two cars)	$ 700
entertainment	$ 600
gifts	$ 85
charitable donations	$ 125
gas and car maintenance	$ 750
total monthly expenses	$7,517

The formula would look like this:

Total monthly expenses + 5% total monthly expenses = total annual expenses (minus housing)

Adding the columns, we get:

$7,517 + $375.85 (5% of total monthly expenses) = $7,892.85 total monthly expenses (minus housing)

Other Assets

Next, to determine the nature of the mortgage loan the buyer will require, it's important to know the buyer's net worth, how much additional money the buyer has, and how much of that money is readily accessible for a down payment. Included in these calculations is money in savings and money market accounts, checking accounts, retirement funds, stocks, bonds, mutual fund investments, and other savings. If the buyer owns a home, add in the estimated selling price of the home and subtract the amount of the balance of the mortgage.

> *Other Assets Example:*
> Again, following our couple along, they do not own a home, but they do have the following assets:

> | | |
> |---|---:|
> | savings/money market account | $ 5,000 |
> | checking account | $ 3,250 |
> | retirement fund contributions | $50,000 |
> | stocks, bonds, and mutual fund investments | $25,000 |
> | other savings | $10,000 |
> | | $93,250 |

CALCULATING DEBT RATIOS

Once income and expenses have been calculated, to determine how much debt a borrower can afford to pay for housing, most lenders use debt ratios, including a housing expense ratio or a total obligations ratio. For most conventional mortgages, the housing expense ratio can be no higher than 28% and the total obligations ratio can be no higher than 36%. FHA uses 29% and 41%.

> *Debt Ratio Example 1:*
> The formula for the housing expense ratio is:
> PITI ÷ monthly gross income = housing expense ratio
> Using the gross income of our couple, let's assume they've found a $200,000 home and would like to put down 15%. $200,000 × .15 = $30,000 down. $200,000 minus $30,000 would mean a $170,000 mortgage. At 6.5% interest on a 30-year fixed-rate loan, monthly payments would be $1,074.51 for principal and interest. Property taxes are estimated at $350, and insurance will add to another $90 per month.

Begin by adding:

$1,074.51 + $350 + $90 = $1,514.51

$1,514.51 (PITI) ÷ $16,804.17 (monthly income) = .0901 or 9.01%

Next, add in other long-term expenses, $1,000 per month repayment of student loans and $700 per month in car payments. The formula for the total obligations ratio is:

PITIO ÷ monthly gross income = total obligations ratio

PITIO = $1,514.51 + $1,700 = $3,214.51

$2,214.51 ÷ $16,804.17 = 0.13178, or 13.2%

13.2% is less than the required back-end ratio of 36% for a conventional loan or 41% for an FHA loan.

Debt Ratio Example 2:

To determine the maximum dollar amount PITI for a conventional mortgage:

$16,804.17 × .28 = $4,705.17 front-end qualifier

($16,804.17 × .36) − $1,700 =

$6,049.50 − $1,700 = $4,349.50 back-end qualifier

Lenders generally go with the lower of the two numbers as the maximum PITI.

PUT YOUR DEBT RATIO CALCULATION SKILLS TO WORK

1. A borrower wants to know if she qualifies for an FHA mortgage. Her monthly income is $6,500, estimated PITI is $2,500, and her car payment is $400 per month.

2. In dollars, what is the maximum PITI someone with an income of $150,000 and long-term debt of $22,000 per year could qualify for if applying for an FHA mortgage?

TYPES OF MORTGAGES

There are many types of mortgages, among them fixed-rate 15-, 20-, 25-, and 30-year mortgages, adjustable rate mortgages (ARMs), growing equity mortgages (GEMs), graduated payment mortgages (GPMs), interest-only mortgages, Federal Housing Administration (FHA) mortgages, Veterans' Administration (VA) mortgages, and, in rural areas, Farm Service Agency (FSA) mortgages. They meet different needs and have different advantages and disadvantages. Some mortgages are assumable, others are not.

Things that affect a mortgage payment amount and mortgage calculations are the size of the down payment, which affects the amount borrowed (principal) and the type of loan available; points (the cost of borrowing); property taxes; and insurance. Principal, interest, taxes, and insurance are the four major components of a mortgage payment. Real estate professionals will find themselves comparing different types of mortgages to find the one that's right for their clients and/or their own investing needs.

In this chapter, we'll review the most common forms of mortgages and the mathematical computations associated with them.

TRADITIONAL/FIXED-RATE CONVENTIONAL MORTGAGE

The fixed-rate mortgage is the industry standard, and, for this reason, it is known as a conventional loan. Generally, traditional fixed-rate mortgages have a term of 30 years, and payments are predictable and spread over a long period. Today, borrowers can find fixed-rate mortgages for periods as few as 15 years and as long as 40 years.

▶ *Tip*

The fewer the number of years, the lower the interest rate, the higher the monthly payment, the lower the tax deduction, and the faster the equity builds.

These loans conform to the limits set by Fannie Mae and Freddie Mac, the two largest secondary markets for mortgage loans. The limit in 2007 is $417,000 for single-family residences, except in Alaska, Hawaii, Guam, and the U.S. Virgin Islands, where the maximum amount is $625,500.

▶ *Tip*

The conforming limits refer to the amount of the mortgage, not the selling price of the home.

Fixed-Rate Math

Twenty percent of the home's purchase price as a down payment was once standard. That is no longer true. Loans for much less than 20% down are available. If the down payment is less than 20%, most lenders demand that the purchaser buy private mortgage insurance (PMI), which protects the lender in the event of default. In some cases, the lender will accept a higher rate of interest in lieu of mortgage insurance when the down payment is less than 20%. PMI rates vary, but are in the neighborhood of .5% to 1% of the loan.

The down payment is a percentage of the actual selling price of the property. The formula is simple.

down payment = selling price × % required

Thus, if the selling price of a condominium is $250,000, and the lender requires a 20% down payment, the calculation is:

250,000 × 20% (or .2) = $50,000

With a 5% down payment, the equation would look like this:

250,000 × 5% (or .05) = $12,500

Typically, the first year's PMI payment is required at closing. Therefore, if mortgage insurance is required, the equation looks like this:

down payment + (loan amount × % PMI required) = amount due

▶ *Tip*

Do the math inside the parenthesis before proceeding to the rest of the calculation.

Let's assume the selling price of a home is $305,000, the purchaser is putting 10% down, and the rate for PMI is .5% (.005). To determine the amount the buyer would need at closing, break the equation down into its parts. Start with the down payment:

down payment = 305,000 × .1 = $30,500

Subtract the down payment from the selling price:

loan amount = 305,000 − 30,500 = $274,500

▶ *Tip*

Another way to calculate the amount of loan is to multiply by 90% (.9). The equation would be 305,000 × .9 = $274,500.

Next, calculate the PMI due:

$274,500 × .005 = $1,372.50

Add the results:

$30,500 + $1,372.50 = $31,872.50

Note: Other fees will be needed in cash at the closing; we'll discuss these in Chapter 11.

Interest-Only Mortgage

An interest-only mortgage is a relatively recent option. The name says it all: The borrower pays only interest on the loan and no principal for a specified period, usually five to ten years. This type of mortgage makes sense for those who do not intend to hold the property for more than a few years.

Interest-Only Mortgage Example:

If a 30-year loan of $100,000 at 6.25% is interest-only, the required payment is $520.83. After that period, the payment increases to include payment of the principal. Additionally, depending upon whether the interest rate of the loan was fixed or adjustable, the interest rate could increase. Most interest-only loans are also adjustable rate.

The identical fixed-rate mortgage would require a monthly payment of $615.72. The difference of $94.88 goes toward repaying the "principal" on the loan of a fixed-rate mortgage.

Jumbo Mortgages

Loans for more than the conforming loan amount of $417,000 (in 2007) are considered "jumbo," and lenders must find secondary lenders on Wall Street and elsewhere to purchase these loans. For this reason, interest rates on jumbo mortgages tend to be .25% to .5% higher than other mortgages. A higher down payment, approximately 5%, is usually required, and no-money-down programs are generally not available. Because the loans are large, adjustable rate mortgages are popular because of the lower monthly payment.

 ▶ *Tip*

As home prices rose in many parts of the country, especially between 2004 and 2006, more mortgages moved into the jumbo category. To meet the need for mortgages in this area, the rules are changing. For example, some borrowers now take a second mortgage at a slightly higher interest, as a way to avoid PMI, which is costly on a large mortgage. To see how this works, see Chapter 5.

Seller Carrybacks

Seller carrybacks are when credit is extended by the seller to the buyer and security is held by the seller of the property. Often when doing a seller carryback, the equity is low. They are second mortgages, if they are repaid *after* the original mortgage lender. Second mortgages carry greater risk, because if there is a default, the holder of the first mortgage will be paid first. Only if there is money left will the holder of the second mortgage be paid.

Interest rates on seller carrybacks are a matter of negotiation between the seller and the buyer. As with other mortgages, the amount of the down payment and the buyer's creditworthiness are key factors. On the other hand, if the buyer had cash and great credit, he or she would probably not ask for a seller carryback. Sometimes, sellers agree to carrybacks in difficult markets or when they don't need the cash out right away; sometimes, they can receive a higher selling price in return for a seller carryback.

Generally, seller carrybacks may be 8% to 12% for between five and ten years. A typical arrangement may be 10% down, 10% seller carryback, and an 80% first mortgage. The mortgage is calculated in the same way as other fixed-rate mortgages.

PUT YOUR FIXED-RATE MATH SKILLS TO WORK

3. The purchase price of a house is $475,500. How much would a buyer need for a down payment of 20%?

4. The buyer is putting 15% down, the PMI is .75%, and the selling price of the house is $247,500. Calculate the amount of cash the buyer will need.

5. The purchase price of a home is $267,000. How much down payment would the buyer need if the first mortgage is 80% and the carryback is 7.5%?

VA AND FHA MORTGAGES

Both VA and FHA mortgages are federally backed mortgages obtained from traditional lenders.

VA Mortgages

VA loans are available only to veterans, surviving spouses, and active military personnel. A VA loan guarantee is not an automatic benefit; the VA offers a guarantee only on loans that meet the requirements, which include borrowers with a good credit rating, a maximum debt ratio of 41%, and the requisite income to handle house payments. To apply, a certificate of eligibility is required.

The VA does not issue loans; it guarantees the loan. Loans are made by private lenders, such as banks, savings and loans, or mortgage companies. To get a loan, a veteran must apply to a lender. If the loan is approved, the VA will guarantee a portion of it to the lender. This guaranty protects the lender against loss up to the amount guaranteed and allows a veteran to obtain favorable financing terms.

There is no maximum amount for a VA loan, but the VA will limit the amount it will guarantee. The amount of the guarantee changes annually. For loans up to this amount, it is usually possible for qualified veterans to obtain financing with no money down if the veteran is income- and credit-qualified and if the property appraises for the asking price.

In 2007, the maximum guarantee authorized by the VA was 25% of the loan amount up to $104,250. The maximum home loan that the VA will guarantee is $417,000. For properties in Hawaii, Guam, Alaska, and the U.S. Virgin Islands, loan limits can be up to $625,000, where the maximum loan guarantee is $256,250.

Types of VA Mortgages

The VA will guarantee a variety of mortgage types, including:

- traditional fixed payment
- graduated payment mortgage (GPMs)
- growing equity mortgages (GEMs)
- adjustable rate mortgages (ARMs), where annual adjustments are limited to 1% and the maximum interest rate increase over the life of the loan is limited to 5%
- hybrid ARMs, where the initial rate remains fixed for at least three years

However, funding fees (a percentage of the total home loan) must be paid to the VA at time of closing. Some expenses (over and above the price of the property) incurred by buyers in transferring ownership of a property must also be paid out of pocket.

Among the advantages of VA guaranteed loans are:

- no down payment in most cases; unlike private mortgages, PMI is not required
- loan maximum may be up to 100% of the VA-established reasonable value of the property; however, loans generally may not exceed limits set by the VA each year

- interest rates may be negotiated with the lender
- limitation on buyer's closing costs

Funding fees may be higher for veterans who previously used the VA home loan program.

FHA 203(b) Mortgage

FHA mortgages are designed for low- and moderate-income families. Mortgage lending limits vary based on the type of housing as well as the state and county in which the property is located. There are higher limits for two- to four-family properties. FHA offers traditional fixed-rate mortgages as well as ARMs, GEMs, and other mortgages.

FHA Title II Section 203(b) is the most popular FHA program. It can be used to purchase new or existing one- to four-family homes, including manufactured homes, in both urban and rural areas. A section 203(b) fixed-rate mortgage is a 15- or 30-year fixed-rate mortgage.

Interest rates on FHA loans are slightly higher than market rates; however, the down payment is lower, but must be *at least* 3%. Closing costs may be included in the mortgage and may be counted toward that 3% minimum.

▶ *FHA Maximum Loan-to-Value Percentages*

Low Closing Costs States*
- 98.75%: For properties with value or sales price** equal to or less than $50,000
- 97.65%: For properties with value or sales price in excess of $50,000 up to $125,000
- 97.15%: For properties with value or sales price in excess of $125,000

High Closing Costs States
- 98.75%: For properties with value or sales price equal to or less than $50,000
- 97.75%: For properties with value or sales price in excess of $50,000

* All but 25 states and territories are considered high closing cost states. A list can be found at http://www.hudclips.org/sub_nonhud/cgi/pdfforms/98-29attach.pdf.
** Value – appraised value; loan is based on the lower of the two.

FHA Example:

The calculation to determine how much one can borrow is

sale price × % available = maximum FHA loan amount

Thus, if the sale price is $75,000, the calculation is

$75,000 × 97.75% =

$75,000 × .9775 = $73,312.50 maximum FHA loan amount

To determine the minimum cash investment, simply multiply the sales price by 3% (.03). In the previous example,

$75,000 × .03 = $2,250

The total acquisition cost is equal to the sales price plus the closing costs that are paid by the buyer. If closing costs are $1,000, the calculation for total acquisition cost is $75,000 sales price + $1,000 closing costs = $76,000 total acquisition costs.

To see if this purchase meets the minimum cash investment requirement, subtract $73,312.50 from $76,000:

$76,000 − $73,312.50 = $2,687.50 down payment

Because this is more than the required minimum cash investment of $2,250, the down payment of $2,687.50 is sufficient. Had it been less than the minimum required cash amount, the amount of the loan would have been reduced by the difference.

Note: FHA loans are always rounded to the nearest $50. In this case, $73,312.50 is rounded to $73,300, which decreases the buyer's down payment by $12.50.

PUT YOUR VA AND FHA CALCULATION SKILLS TO WORK

6. Assume the appraised value and the selling price of a home purchased with a guaranteed loan from the VA is $312,000. How much of the loan will the VA guarantee?

7. Assuming the scenario in question 6 is a first purchase and the funding fee is .5%, how much will the funding fee be?

8. Assume that the appraised value and the selling price was $160,000 in a low-closing-cost state, and that the closing costs are $325. Calculate the total FHA mortgage.

9. In question 8, does the buyer meet the required minimum cash investment?

ADJUSTABLE RATE MORTGAGE (ARM)

As the name implies, the interest rate on ARMs mirrors the fluctuations in interest rates. Generally, the initial rate of interest is low—an incentive for the borrower in exchange for potential higher rates if and when interest rates go up. Interest rates on ARMs are adjusted periodically; some are adjusted annually, others every few years as specified in the mortgage agreement.

The index to which the ARM is pegged can dramatically affect the loan's volatility. For this reason, most mortgage agreements contain caps on the amount the interest rate can increase at any one time. Some ARMs include a cap on the amount a payment can increase over the life of the mortgage. There are three types of caps: initial adjustment caps, periodic adjustment caps, and lifetime caps. These are usually represented as three numbers, such as 1/2/6. The first is the initial adjustment, in this case, 1%; the second, the periodic adjustment, 2%; and last, the lifetime cap, 6%.

To estimate the cost of an ARM, several things must be considered:

- the amount of the loan, and the interest rates over the life of the mortgage
- the length of the mortgage
- the intervals between adjustments

Once one knows this information, the equations are identical to those used to calculate the cost of a fixed-rate mortgage. However, the math is cumbersome because one also has to compute the amount of principal on which interest was being paid.

▶ *Tip*

Here are some of the many mortgage calculators available online:
http://fha.com/calculator_amortization.cfm
http://www.mtgprofessor.com/calculators.htm
http://www.fincalc.com/hom_11.asp?id=6
http://www.gmacmortgage.com/calculators.do?method=mortgage
Adjustable
http://www.bankofamerica.com/loansandhomes/index.cfm?template=
learn_calculators&context=financenter&calcid=home04

GROWING EQUITY MORTGAGE (GEM)

This type of loan, normally a 30-year mortgage, features a fixed rate and a changing monthly payment pegged to an index. Unlike an ARM, when the payment goes up, the excess goes to pay down principal, not to additional interest payments. This allows the borrower to pay off the loan more rapidly than he or she can with a traditional fixed-rate mortgage.

These are a bit easier to calculate than ARMs, but here, too, one of the many online calculators may be better.

ANSWERS

Answers appear in **boldface**.

1. **No,** maximum FHA ratios are 29% for housing expense and 41% for all debt including housing.

   $2,500 ÷ $6,500 = .3846 housing expense

   ($2,500 + $400) ÷ $6,500 = **.4462 total debt**, which exceeds the permitted 41%

2. $150,000 (annual income) ÷ 12 = $12,500 monthly income

   $22,000 (annual long-term debt) ÷ 12 = $1,833.33 monthly debt

   $12,500 × .29 = $3,625 maximum housing expense

   ($12,500 × .41) – $1,833.33 =

   $5,125 – $1,833.33 = **$3,291.67**

3. $475,500 × .2 = **$95,100**

4. down payment required + (loan amount × % PMI required) = amount due

   $247,500 × .15 = $37,125 = down payment

   $247,500 – $37,125 = $210,375 = amount of loan

   $210,375 × .0075 = $1,577.81 (rounded) = PMI

   $37,125 + $1,577.81 = **$38,702.81** amount due

5. 80% + 7.5% = 87.5% (amount borrowed both loans)

   $267,000 × .125 = **$33,375** down payment

6. $312,000 (purchase price) × .25 = **$78,000** (amount guaranteed by VA)

7. $312,000 × .5% = funding fee

   $312,000 × .005 = **$1,560** funding fee

8. $160,000 × 97.15% =

   160,000 × .9715 = **$155,440** maximum FHA loan amount

9. **Yes**, the buyer meets the minimum cash investment.

   $160,000 × .03 = $4,800 minimum cash investment

   $160,325 – $155,440 = $4,885 down payment

BASIC MORTGAGE CALCULATIONS

Whether a property is purchased for personal use or as an investment, it is a large purchase that often requires financing. Mortgage calculations involve the *principal* (*P*), which is the amount of money borrowed; the *rate of interest* (*R*), the cost of the money and the annual percentage that is being charged for the loan; and *time* (*T*), which refers to the duration of the loan as well as the periodic payment schedule. We'll examine the calculations involved in each of these and finish the chapter by seeing how they work together.

▶ *Before You Begin, You Need to Know . . .*

The mathematic formulas that express the relationship among the components in a mortgage calculation are:

$$I = P \times R \times T \qquad P = \frac{I}{R \times T} \qquad R = \frac{I}{P \times T} \qquad T = \frac{I}{P \times R}$$

Total Monthly Payment = Principal + Interest + Taxes + Insurance (known as PITI)

CALCULATING THE INTEREST ON ANY LOAN

Although interest on mortgages is generally paid monthly, the lender most often presents the rate in yearly terms, such as 6.25% per year. The lender will also provide an annual percentage rate (APR), which is the interest rate plus any associated fees, which may include the following:

- points—both discount points and origination points (see Chapter 4)
- prepaid interest—the interest paid from the date the loan closes to the end of the month, usually assumed to be 15 days when presenting APRs (see Chapter 4)
- loan processing fee (see Chapter 11)
- underwriting fee (see Chapter 11)
- document preparation fee (see Chapter 11)
- private mortgage insurance (PMI) (see Chapters 2 and 5)
- loan application fee (see Chapter 11)

▶ *Tip*

Not all lenders include the same fees in their interest rates, so when comparing APRs, be sure to determine what is and is not included.

Interest Example:

Let's assume you borrow $100,000 at this rate for one year. To determine how much you owe each year, the calculation would be:

$I = P \times R \times T$

$= 100{,}000 \times 6.25\% \times 1 \text{ year}$

$= 100{,}000 \times .0625 \times 1$

$= \$6{,}250$

If you wanted to find your monthly payment, the formula would be the same, but the calculation would look like this:

$= 100{,}000 \times 6.25\% \times \frac{1}{12} \text{ year}$

$= 100{,}000 \times .0625 \times \frac{1}{12}$

$= 6{,}250 \times .0833$

$= \$520.83 \text{ (rounded) per month}$

▶ Tip

As you've no doubt noticed, you could simply have divided the answer in the first calculation by 12. So, if you already know that number, you can jump directly to the last step.

To obtain the daily interest, you would divide by 365:

$= 6{,}250 \div 365$

$= \$17.12$

▶ Tip

Some states use a 360-day year/30-day method. In that case, the formulas are:

daily interest = annual interest ÷ 360 days

monthly interest = annual interest ÷ 12 months

We'll be using the 365-day system throughout this book, unless otherwise noted.

There are times, such as closings, when you must calculate interest to the day.

Daily Interest Example:

How much would you owe on $175,000 if the interest rate were 7.25% for seven months and three days?

1. Calculate annual interest: $175,000 × .0725 = $12,687.50
2. Calculate monthly interest: $12,687.50 ÷ 12 = $1,057.29
3. Calculate daily interest: $12,687.50 ÷ 365 = $34.76

To find the amount owed

4. Calculate seven months' interest: 7 × 1,057.29 = $7,401.03
5. Calculate three days' interest: 3 × $34.76 = $104.28
6. Add the results of steps 4 and 5: $7,401.03

$$\begin{array}{r} \$7,401.03 \\ +\ \ 104.28 \\ \hline \$7,505.41 \end{array}$$

► *Tip*

When you are computing interest, the result will be more accurate if you carry the answer to at least three decimal places and then round off the final answer.

PUT YOUR INTEREST CALCULATION SKILLS TO WORK

1. On a $250,000 loan with an interest rate of 7.2%, how much are the annual payments?

2. How much would you owe on a $475,000 loan at 6.75% for 15 days?

CALCULATING THE IMPACT OF TIME ON ANY LOAN

Thus far, all of our calculations have been based on the formula $I = P \times R \times T$, where the amount of time was one year or a fraction of it. If you are looking at interest over a longer period, or if one of the elements is missing, using the multistep method previously described would be cumbersome. Using one of the other equations provides the solution.

Impact of Time Example 1:

Let's assume you have a fixed-rate 30-year mortgage locked in at 5.75%, and you paid $22,500 interest in the last six months. How much did you borrow?

▶ *Tip*

Before you begin, convert six months into a decimal or fraction.

$\frac{6 \text{ months}}{12 \text{ months}} = \frac{\text{part}}{\text{whole}} - \frac{1}{2}$ or 0.5.

Begin with the formula $P = \frac{I}{R \times T}$

$\quad = \frac{22{,}500}{.0575 \times .5}$

$\quad = 22{,}500 \div (.0575 \times .5)$

$\quad = 22{,}500 \div .0288$

$\quad = \$781{,}250$

Impact of Time Example 2:

Similarly, if you don't know the rate of interest, but know the amount paid over a certain period of time, you can determine the rate by using the formula:

$R = \frac{I}{P \times T}$

Using the facts from the previous example, calculate the rate of interest as follows:

$\quad = \frac{22{,}500}{782{,}608.70}$

$\quad = 22{,}500 \div (782{,}608.70 \times .5)$

$\quad = 22{,}500 \div 391{,}305$

$\quad = 0.0575$

Note: The difference of .0001 is the result from rounding in the original example to determine the length of the loan. Let's use .0575 as the rate of interest.

The formula is:

$T = \frac{I}{P \times R}$

▶ *Tip*

Before you begin, multiply \$22,500, which represents six months of payments, by 60 payments to get the total amount paid over the life of the mortgage.

$\quad = \frac{22{,}500 \times 60}{781{,}250 \times .0575}$

$\quad = (22{,}500 \times 60) \div (781{,}250 \times .0575)$

$\quad = 1{,}350{,}000 \div 44{,}921.875$

$\quad = 30.05$ years

Note: The difference of .05 is the result of rounding in previous calculations.

PUT YOUR TIME CALCULATION SKILLS TO WORK

3. Let's assume you have a fixed-rate 25-year mortgage and your interest rate is 7.5%. In the first three months of the year, you paid $3,000 interest. How much did you borrow?

4. Find the rate of interest on a loan of $150,000 if the amount of interest paid after two years is $26,500.

5. Find the term of a $175,000 loan where the rate of interest is 8.5% and $60,000 has been paid.

CALCULATING EARNEST MONEY AND DOWN PAYMENT

Earnest money, also known as a "binder" or "good faith deposit," is money a buyer puts down to demonstrate his or her seriousness about buying a home. Laws and customs vary from state to state, but in general, the amount should be large enough to demonstrate serious interest. In "hot" markets, the amount may be higher as an indication of the buyer's enthusiasm for a particular house.

A down payment is the amount paid when the contract is signed, and it too is applied toward the buyer's down payment. It generally is made in cash. The amount varies, but as a rule, it is between 5% and 20% of the purchase price. An additional amount may be needed to satisfy mortgage requirements. During the "hot" real estate market of the early 2000s, which saw property values rise exponentially in many parts of the country, the necessary down payment amount was lowered to as little as 3%, and, in some cases, no down payment was required.

Earnest money is the amount paid when the contract is signed. A down payment is the amount paid before the transaction closes. Earnest money becomes part of the down payment if the offer is accepted and is held in escrow until closing. If the offer is rejected, the money is returned. On occasion, if the buyer later backs away from the deal, some or all of the amount is forfeited.

► *Tip*

When an individual purchases an investment property, the risk to the lender is thought to increase, and the down payment as well as the rate of interest may be higher than if the property were purchased as an owner-occupied residence.

Earnest Money/Down Payment Example:

To calculate earnest money and down payment if the purchase price is $75,000 and the buyer is paying 1% as earnest money and a 7.5% additional down payment, calculate the amounts separately: Multiply 1% × 75,000 = $750 earnest money; then multiply .075 × 75,000 = $5,625 down payment. To calculate the total, add 1% + 7.5% = 8.5% and multiply .085 × 75,000 = $6,375, or simply add $750 + $5,625 = $6,375.

PUT YOUR EARNEST MONEY/DOWN PAYMENT CALCULATION SKILLS TO WORK

6. Assume that a borrower is purchasing the "perfect" townhouse, has paid 2.5% as earnest money to be applied toward the down payment, and has made an additional down payment of 10% on contract signing. The townhouse sales price is $425,000. Assume, too, that the buyer is taking an 80% conventional mortgage. Excluding other closing costs, how much does the buyer have to bring to the closing to satisfy mortgage requirements?

ANSWERS

Answers appear in **boldface**.

1. $I = P\ (\$250{,}000) \times R\ (7.2\%) \times T\ (1\ \text{year})$
$= \$250{,}000 \times 7.2\% \times 1$
$= \$250{,}000 \times .072 \times 1$
$= \mathbf{\$18{,}000}$

2. $I = P\ (\$475{,}000) \times R\ (6.75\%) \times T\ (1\ \text{year})$
$= \$475{,}000 \times 6.75\% \times 1$
$= \$475{,}000 \times .0675 \times 1$
$= \$32{,}062.50$
$\$32{,}062.50 \div 365 = \$87.84\ (\text{daily interest})$
$\$87.84 \times 15 = \mathbf{\$1{,}317.60}$

3. $P = \dfrac{I\ (\$3{,}000)}{R\ (7.5\%) \times T\ (3\ \text{months})}$
$= \dfrac{3{,}000}{7.5\% \times .25}$
$= \$3{,}000 \div (.075 \times .25)$
$= \$3{,}000 \div .01875$
$= \mathbf{\$160{,}000}$

4. $R = \dfrac{I\ (\$26{,}500)}{P\ (\$150{,}000) \times T\ (2\ \text{years})}$
$= \dfrac{\$26{,}500}{\$150{,}000 \times 2}$
$= \dfrac{\$26{,}500}{\$300{,}000}$
$= \$26{,}500 \div \$300{,}000$
$= \mathbf{.088}\ \text{or}\ \mathbf{8.8\%}$

5. $T = \dfrac{I\,(\$60,000)}{P\,(\$175,000) \times R\,(8.5\%)}$

$= \dfrac{\$60,000}{\$175,000 \times .085}$

$= \$60,000 \div (\$175,000 \times .085)$

$= \$60,000 \div 14,875 = 0.0336$

$= $ **4.0336** or **4 years, 12 days**

6. $2.5\% + 10\% = 12.5\%$

$\$425,000 \times .125 = \$53,125$ amount paid prior to closing

$\$425,000 \times .2 = \$85,000$

$\$85,000 - \$53,125 = $ **$31,875** due at closing

4

ADVANCED MORTGAGE CALCULATIONS

▶ *Before You Begin, You*
Need to Know . . .

---

1 discount point = 1% of the loan

Each discount point lowers the rate by $\frac{1}{8}$ of 1%, or .00125.

CALCULATING DISCOUNT POINTS AND ORIGINATION FEES

An origination fee (or point) is the fee paid to the company originating your loan to cover the costs associated with creating, processing, and closing your mortgage. This charge amounts to approximately 1% of the loan amount. Often, origination fees are built into the loan amount. Discount points differ from origination fees in that discount points are used to reduce the interest rate on a mortgage.

Discount points are essentially prepaid interest. Each discount point is an upfront payment of 1% of the loan amount, paid at closing. In theory, because the lender has received this money upfront, the borrower obtains a lower interest rate in exchange; today, however, lenders charge points to increase their profits, and the points could be considered an additional payment to the lender. Regardless of how points are viewed, the amount should be factored into the borrowing decision, because it affects the effective rate of the loan.

▶ *Tip*

Lenders base discount points on the size of the loan, not the price of the house.

Although there is no hard and fast rule, on average each discount point paid on a 30-year loan lowers the interest rate by $\frac{1}{8}$ of 1% (.00125). A 7.5% rate would be lowered to 7.375% if the borrower purchased one point (.075 − .00125 =.07375).

Assuming there is a choice, deciding whether paying points is good for the borrower depends upon the length of time he or she plans to own the property. To determine this, you must calculate the break-even point. To determine the break-even point, you need to know the:

- original interest rate
- rate after discount points
- number of discount points
- total amount of the loan
- term of the loan

Break-Even Example:
$100,000 loan with a 30-year term
7.5% interest, no points = $699.21 monthly payment
Buying one point for $1,000 = monthly payment $690.68
Monthly savings = $8.53
$1,000 ÷ $8.53 = 117 months
The break-even point is 117 months—or nearly ten years to recover the cost of buying the discount point (considering only the simple calculation of those funds at today's value).
If the buyer plans to keep the house that long, purchasing one point may make sense, but most homebuyers do not keep their homes that long. The national average is between five and seven years.

► *Tip*

To perform this calculation, use an amortization schedule. You can create one either manually or with a spreadsheet program or calculator, which can be cumbersome if you are working with a long time frame. Or you can use a mortgage calculator or refer to an existing amortization schedule. You can find this information on many websites, including:

http://fha.com/calculator_amortization.cfm

www.mtgprofessor.com/calculators.htm

www.fincalc.com/hom_11.asp?id=6

www.gmacmortgage.com/calculators.do?method=mortgageAdjustable

www.bankofamerica.com/loansandhomes/index.cfm?template=learn
_calculators&context=financenter&calcid=home04

PUT YOUR BREAK-EVEN CALCULATION SKILLS TO WORK

1. Let's assume the buyer in the break-even example decided to take a 15-year mortgage. Using a mortgage calculator, find out if the buyer does better or worse than in the example.

2. Let's assume the loan was for $500,000 at the same rate on a 15-year mortgage. How long would it take the borrower to break even?

► *Tip*

Mortgage calculators also provide the total amount of interest a borrower would pay over the life of the mortgage. The total interest paid on a $500,000 loan over 15 years at 7.5% would be $334,311.12; the same loan over 30 years would cost $758,586.12, or $424,275 more. Of course, this calculation doesn't factor in tax consequences, the value of money, and so on.

Origination fees and points can be used to compare market rates and FHA rates, as well as to calculate the cost of points. In doing these calculations, the important thing to remember is that every point reduces the interest rate by $\frac{1}{8}$ of 1% and that every point is the equivalent of one percentage point.

Comparing Rates Example:

If the rate on a fixed-rate 30-year mortgage is $6\frac{1}{4}$%, the FHA rate is $5\frac{1}{8}$%, and the amount to be borrowed is $111,000, the calculation is:

$$6\frac{1}{4} - 5\frac{1}{8} =$$
$$6\frac{2}{8} - 5\frac{1}{8} = 1\frac{1}{8}$$

Next, convert the difference to eighths of a percent.

$$1\frac{1}{8}\% = \frac{9}{8}\%$$

Convert the eighths to discount points by dividing.

$$\frac{9}{8}\% \div \frac{1}{8}\% = 9 \text{ discount points needed to obtain equivalent rate}$$

Calculating Costs Example:

Using the previous example, begin this calculation by converting the number of points into a percentage.

$$\frac{9}{8} \div \frac{1}{8} =$$
$$\frac{9}{8} \div \frac{8}{1} =$$
$$\frac{9}{1} =$$

9 points = 9%

Next, multiply this number by the amount of the loan to determine how much the discount cost.

$$\$111{,}000 \times .09 = \$9{,}990$$

PUT YOUR POINT CALCULATION SKILLS TO WORK

3. A borrower who wants to borrow $225,000 has been offered a rate of 5.5%, and is charged two points. What is the cost to the borrower?

4. If an FHA lender will lend a borrower $137,500 for a rate of $5\frac{1}{4}$% on a 15-year fixed-rate mortgage, the conventional rate is $6\frac{1}{2}$%. How many points must the conventional lender charge to meet the FHA rate?

CALCULATING AN AMORTIZATION SCHEDULE

This is a cumbersome process, and anyone with access to the Internet or a good spreadsheet program does not have to suffer through it. On the other hand, doing it yourself will help you understand what it is and why it is so useful.

When a mortgage or any loan is amortized, it is gradually reduced through regular payments—the monthly mortgage. Therefore, to create a schedule, you need to know:

- the principal
- the rate of interest
- the amount of each payment (generally monthly)

To create an amortization schedule, you need to use three formulas:

principal × interest rate ÷ 12 = first month's interest

monthly mortgage payment − first month's interest = principal paid

opening principal balance − principal paid = principal balance due

The schedule should look like this:

AMORTIZATION SCHEDULE: 30 YEARS TO REPAY $400,000 AT 6.25%				
Payment Number	Payment Amount	Interest Amount	Principal Reduction	Balance Due
1	$2,462.87	2,083.33	379.54	399,620.46
2				
3				
4				
5				

Amortization Example 1:

Using the three formulas, let's see how the first payment was derived.

$400,000 (principal) × 6.25% ÷ 12 = first month's interest

$400,000 × .0625 = $25,000 ÷ 12 = $2,083.33

$2,462.87 (monthly mortgage payment) − $2,083.33 (first month's interest) = $379.54 (principal paid)

$400,000 (opening principal balance) − $379.54 (principal paid) = $399,620.46 (principal balance due)

PUT YOUR AMORTIZATION CALCULATION SKILLS TO WORK

Let's assume we want to take a longer view to find out how much interest was paid on this $400,000 loan after 20 years. We know the monthly payment is $2,462.87.

5. Calculate payment 2.

6. Calculate payment 3.

Calculating Amortization in the Long Term

To continue the calculation, you could simply repeat the three formulas as often as necessary. Calculating the entire amortization schedule on a 30-year mortgage by hand would require 360 entries (12 months × 30 years). Quite a bit of work!

Assuming you have or can get all the information, there is an easier way to go, even if an amortization table or online mortgage calculator isn't handy. For example, if you want to determine the amount of interest paid after a given length of time, you must know the monthly payment, the amount of time, the percentage of principal already paid, and the total amount of the mortgage. Then all that's required are four formulas:

- number of years × months in a year = number of payments
- monthly mortgage payment × number of months paid = amount paid to date
- total mortgage amount × percent of loan repaid = amount of loan repaid
- amount repaid − principal paid = interest paid to date

▶ *Tip*

To eliminate a step, combine the first two steps:

number of years × months in a year × monthly mortgage payment = total paid

Amortization Example 2:

Assume that after making payments on that $400,000 mortgage for 20 years, 55% of the principal has been paid. We know the mortgage payment is $2,462.87 each month. To determine how much interest has been paid, begin by multiplying, using the first three formulas:

20 years × 12 months = 240 months paid

$2,462.87 (monthly mortgage payment) × 240 = $591,088.80 total paid to date

$400,000 (total mortgage amount) × .55 (percent of loan repaid) = $220,000 = amount of loan repaid

$591,088.80 − $220,000 = $371,088.80 interest paid to date

PUT YOUR LONG-TERM AMORTIZATION CALCULATION SKILLS TO WORK

7. Assume you took out a $97,500 30-year mortgage 5 years ago. The interest rate is 10% and your monthly payment is $855.63. Only 1% of your principal has been paid. How much interest has been paid?

8. On the same $97,500 mortgage, how much interest will be paid at the end of 30 years?

9. Assuming no points and ignoring closing and other costs, if you refinanced the original mortgage for 30 years at 5%, would you pay more or less total interest after 30 years?

The information derived from an amortization table is invaluable. In addition to determining break-even points, amortization tables show the total amount of interest and/or principal paid over any given period.

Payoff Calculations

Accelerated payment options—monthly, weekly, biweekly—can shorten the life of a mortgage as well as reduce the amount of money spent on interest.

To determine the amount of savings, take the monthly payment schedule, and assuming only four weeks in a month, divide your monthly payment by four for weekly payments or two for bimonthly (twice a month or 26 payments a year). The difference goes directly toward paying off principal, and by the end of one year, one month comes off the mortgage.

▶ *Tip*

Some lenders set up special accounts to facilitate this savings, but there is usually a "setup" fee and a "per transaction" fee, which will slightly reduce the amount of savings.

Using the previous amortization formula, you can calculate the impact over time:

principal × interest ÷ 12 = first month's interest

monthly mortgage payment – first month's interest = principal paid

At the end of month 12:

opening principal balance – principal paid = principal balance due

Or, to make longer-term calculations simpler, get the information from your lender and plug it into the long-term formula:

number of years × months in a year × monthly mortgage payment = total paid

total mortgage amount × percent of loan repaid = amount of loan repaid

amount repaid – principal paid = interest paid to date

This may not seem like much at first, because so much of the mortgage payment in the first year is going to repay interest; however, as principal declines, the amount of interest also declines and more of the payment goes toward amortizing principal.

Amortization Example 3:

The impact on a $125,000 30-year mortgage can be quickly compared:

$729.47 (monthly mortgage) × 12 = $8,753.64

($729.47 ÷ 2) × 26 = $364.74 × 26 = $9,483.24

($729.47 ÷ 4) × 52 = $182.37 × 52 = $9,483.24

$9,483.24 – $8,753.64 = $730

Amortizing the mortgage at the end of month 120 (10 years), the principal balance due is $103,900; at the end of 20 years, it is $38,912; at the end of 24.7 years, the mortgage is paid in full; and the amount of interest saved is $28,534.

▶ **Tip**

There are many accelerated payment and prepayment calculators on the Internet, including:

http://www.gmacmortgage.com (then click on Calculators)

http://www.mortgageintelligence.ca/handy_tools_quick_calculator.aspx

http://www.mortgageintelligence.ca/handy_tools.aspx

PUT YOUR PAYOFF CALCULATION SKILLS TO WORK

AMORTIZATION SCHEDULE: 30 YEARS TO REPAY $400,000 AT 6.25%				
Payment Number	Payment Amount	Interest Amount	Principal Reduction	Balance Due
210	$2,462.87			$207,439
211				
212				

The monthly payment on this mortgage is $2,462.87. At the end of 16 years, the balance due is $207,439.

10. Calculate payment 211.

11. Calculate payment 212.

12. Assume it is now 20 years since this mortgage was taken out, and 70% principal has been paid. How much interest has been paid?

13. How much interest will be paid at the end of 24.3 years, when the mortgage is paid off?

Refinancing Calculations

A borrower must consider a number of things before deciding whether to refinance a mortgage:

- Will the amount saved really compensate for the cost of refinancing?
- Will the borrower benefit from a reduction in monthly payments in exchange for a longer-term mortgage?
- Conversely, if the refinancing is to obtain a shorter-term mortgage, is the long-term saving sufficient to compensate for higher monthly payments?
- If the money is for making a home improvement, will the improvement add to the value of the home equal to or greater than the cost?
- If the money is for another type of investment, such as an investment in stocks or bonds, is it a sound investment?

This can be a risky path. Whatever the reason, before proceeding it is important to perform this type of cost-benefit analysis.

Refinancing Example:

Figure 4.1 provides a quick basis for comparison (for more on closing fees, see Chapter 11).

Current Mortgage

Current monthly payment:	$2,528.27	Current interest rate:	6.5%
Balance left on mortgage:	$347,117.07	New interest rate:	6%
Years left on current loan:	21	New loan term (in years):	20

Calculating Costs

Points:	2	Cost of points	$6,942.34
Application fee:	$1,000	Credit check:	$30
Attorney's fee (yours):	$1,200	Attorney's fee (lenders):	$750
Title search:	$1,000	Title insurance:	$875
Appraisal fee:	$450	Inspections:	$400
Local fees (taxes, transfers):	$200	Document preparation:	$400
Other:	0		

New Mortgage

New monthly payment:	$2,150.82	Monthly savings:	$377.45
Difference in interest:	$137,172.23	Months to recoup costs:	35.1
Total cost:	$13,247.34		

Figure 4.1

PUT YOUR REFINANCING CALCULATION SKILLS TO WORK

Use the following to answer questions 14–16.

Current Mortgage			
Current monthly payment:	$2,462.87	Current interest rate:	6.25%
Balance left on mortgage:	$275,300.80	New interest rate:	6%
Years left on current loan:	14	New loan term (in years):	20
Calculating Costs			
Points:	2	Cost of points	$6,942.34
Application fee:	$1,000	Credit check:	$30
Attorney's fee (yours):	$1,200	Attorney's fee (lenders):	$750
Title search:	$1,000	Title insurance:	$875
Appraisal fee:	$450	Inspections:	$400
Local fees (taxes, transfers):	$200	Document preparation:	$400
Other:	0		

14. Calculate the amount of interest that would have been paid on the balance of the old mortgage after 14 years.

15. The new monthly payment would be $1,650.47. Calculate the amount of interest that will have been paid on the new mortgage at the end of 20 years.

16. How much would be saved/lost by refinancing, assuming costs remain same?

CALCULATING MORTGAGE CONSTANTS

A mortgage constant (also called a loan constant) is the amount of cash flow needed each year to pay the principal *and* the interest on a mortgage over the term of the mortgage. To determine this amount, you need to know the amount of the loan, the rate of interest, and the term of the mortgage.

Conversely, when the monthly rate of interest is unknown, and you know the mortgage constant, you can determine the rate of interest.

Mortgage Constant Example 1:

To find the mortgage constant for the $125,000, 30-year mortgage (360 payments of $729.47), divide the monthly payment by the total amount of the mortgage.

$729.47 ÷ $125,000 = .0058357

Mortgage Constant Example 2:

Now, let's reverse the example. The mortgage constant is .0058357 on the same $125,000 loan, but you don't know the monthly payment. This time, multiply the amount of the loan by the mortgage constant to determine the monthly payment.

$125,000 × .0058357 = $729.4625 or $729.47 (rounded)

PUT YOUR MORTGAGE CONSTANT CALCULATION SKILLS TO WORK

17. A 15-year mortgage of $257,500 with an interest rate of 6.95% has monthly loan payments of $2,307.29. What is the loan constant?

18. Find the monthly payment on a $625,000, 20-year mortgage, where the loan constant is .0085206.

Calculating Loan-to-Value Ratio

One of the factors lenders consider before they approve a mortgage is the loan-to-value ratio (LTV), which is a measure of risk. The LTV is the loan amount expressed as a percentage of either the purchase price or the appraised value of the property. The higher the LTV, the higher the risk. Therefore, if the mortgage company agrees to the loan, it will probably charge a higher rate of interest, which frequently makes the loan more difficult to qualify for, and/or the lender may require private mortgage insurance, increasing the cost of the mortgage (see Chapter 2). For the same size loan, some lenders require borrowers to have a larger monthly income to qualify for a high LTV mortgage than do borrowers with a low LTV loan.

A high LTV occurs when the mortgage amount is high in relation to the down payment or to the equity in the property. In general, when borrowers make a large cash down payment or have a large equity in a property, they are less likely to default on the mortgage. Borrowers with less equity in a property have less to lose; therefore, any loan for more than 80% is considered to have a high LTV, even if the appraised value is higher than the purchase price!

► **Tip**

Sellers should be concerned about the buyer's LTV. If the appraised value comes in lower than the purchase price, the lender will base the LTV on the lower of the two amounts.

> *LTV Example:*
> LTV is calculated as:
>> amount of mortgage ÷ appraised value or purchase price = LTV
>> $350,000 (mortgage) ÷ $400,000 (appraised value/purchase price) = 87.5%
>
> This loan could be considered risky, and the borrower may need to go back to the bargaining table in order to avoid paying a higher mortgage rate or putting up additional cash. On the other hand,
>> $275,000 (mortgage) ÷ $400,000 (appraised property value) = 68.7%

PUT YOUR LTV CALCULATION SKILLS TO WORK

19. If the purchase price of a home is $77,900 and the mortgage is $62,500, what is the LTV?

20. Calculate the purchase price of a home if the down payment is $32,500 and the LTV is 73%.

CALCULATING TRANSFER TAXES

Some states charge a one-time transfer tax on mortgages, known as an "intangible tax." The rate varies; currently in Georgia the rate is $1.50 per $500 or $.30 per $100. There is also a one-time "documentary stamp tax" on the note. Currently in Nebraska that rate is $2.25 for each $1,000 or $.225 per $100. These rates may be lower in some states and higher in others. These amounts will appear on closing statements in states that levy them.

▶ *Tip*

If the mortgage is assumed, *and* no new mortgage is created, *and* there is no change in the property securing the loan, then no new *intangible* tax is levied. However, the *documentary stamp* tax would still have to be paid on the assumed mortgage.

Transfer Tax Example:

In a state that levies intangible and documentary stamp taxes, the intangible tax rate is $.27 per $100 and the documentary stamp tax rate is $.35 per $100. If the total mortgage is $725,000, to determine how much is owed for each tax, first divide to obtain the number of hundreds on which the tax must be paid.

$725,000 ÷ 100 = 7,500

Then, multiply to get the intangible tax amount.

$7,500 × $.27 = $2,025

Next, multiply to calculate the documentary stamp tax.

$7,500 × $.35 = $2,625

To determine the total tax amount, add the two $2,025 + $2,625 = $4,650.

PUT YOUR TRANSFER TAX CALCULATION SKILLS TO WORK

21. Assume that the borrower has purchased a townhouse for $365,500 and has put 35% down. Calculate the transfer taxes, assuming the intangible tax rate is $.26 per $100 and the documentary stamp tax rate is $.325.

ANSWERS

Answers are in **boldface**.

1. **Worse.**

   $100,000 loan with a 15-year term

   7.5% interest, no points = $927.01 monthly payment

   buying one point for $1,000 = $919.92 monthly payment

   monthly savings = $7.09

   $1,000 ÷ $7.09 = **141** months or **11** years **9** months

2. $500,000 loan with a 15-year term

   7.5% interest, no points = $4,635.06 monthly payment

   buying one point for $1,000 = $4,599.62 monthly payment

   monthly savings = $35.44

   $1,000 ÷ 35.44 = **28.2** months or **2** years **4** months

3. $225,000 × .02 = **$4,500**

4. $6\frac{1}{2}\% - 5\frac{1}{4}\% = 1\frac{1}{4}\%$

   $1\frac{1}{4}\% = \frac{10}{8}\%$

   $\frac{10}{8}\% \div \frac{1}{8} =$ **10** discount points

5. Payment 2:

   $399,620.46 × .0625 ÷ 12 = $2,081.36

   $2,462.87 − $2,081.36 = $381.51

   $399,620.46 − $381.51 = **$399,238.95**

6. Payment 3:

   $399,238.95 × .0625 ÷ 12 = $2,079.37

   $2,462.87 − $2,079.37 = $383.50

   $399,238.95 − $383.50 = **$398,855.45**

7. $855.63 (monthly payment) × 5 (years) × 12 (months) = $51,337.80 (total paid to date)

   $97,500 (total mortgage) × .01 = $975 principal paid

   $97,500 − $975 = **$96,525** interest paid

8. $855.63 × 30 × 12 = $308,026.80 total paid to date

   $308,026 − $97,500 = **$210,526.80** interest paid

9. $523.40 \times 30 \times 12 = \$188,424$ total paid to date

$188,424 - \$97,500 = \$90,924$ interest paid

$90,924 + \$96,525$ (interest paid on previous mortgage) $= \$187,449$ total interest paid

$210,526.80 - \$187,449 = \textbf{\$23,077.80}$ amount saved by refinancing

10. Payment 211:

$207,439 \times .0625 \div 12 = \$1,080.41$

$2,462.87 - \$1,080.41 = \$1,382.46$

$207,439 - \$1,382.46 = \textbf{\$206,056.54}$

11. Payment 212:

$206,056.54 \times .0625 \div 12 = \$1,073.21$

$2,462.87 - \$1,073.21 = \$1,389.66$

$206,056 - \$1,389.66 = \textbf{\$204,666.34}$

12. $2,462.87 \times 20$ (years) $\times 13$ (months) $= \$640,346.20$ total paid to date

$400,000$ (total mortgage) $\times .70 = \$280,000$ principal paid

$640,346.20 - \$280,000 = \textbf{\$360,346.20}$ interest paid

13. $2,462.87 \times 24.3 \times 13 = \$778,020.63$ total paid

$778,020.63 - \$400,000 = \textbf{\$378,020.63}$ interest paid

14. $2,462.87 \times 14$ (years) $\times 12$ (months) $= \$413,762.16$ balance of mortgage

$275,300.80$ principal repaid after 16 years

$413,762.16 - \$275,300.80 = \textbf{\$138,461.36}$ additional interest paid

15. $1,650.47 \times 20$ (years) $\times 12$ (months) $= \$396,112.80$

$396,112.80 - \$275,300.80 = \textbf{\$120,812}$ interest paid

16. $138,461.36 - \$120,812 = \$17,649.36$ interest saved

$17,649.36 - \$13,247.34$ (expenses) $= \textbf{\$4,402.02}$ net savings

17. $2,307.29 \div \$257,500 = \textbf{.0089603}$ mortgage constant

18. $625,000 \times .0085206 = \$5,325.375 = \textbf{\$5,325.38}$ (rounded) monthly payment

19. $62,500$ (mortgage) $\div \$77,900$ (purchase price) $= \textbf{.8}$ or $\textbf{80\%}$ LTV

20. 100% (purchase price) – 73% (loan) = 27% down payment or .27

27% is equal to $32,500 down payment

$32,500 ÷ .27 = x

x = **$120,370.37** purchase price

21. 100% – 35% = 65% financed or .65

$365,500 sales price × .65 financed = $237,575

$237,575 ÷ 100 = $2,375.75 taxable hundreds

$2,375.75 × $.26 = **$617.70** (rounded) intangible tax due

$2,375.75 × $.325 = **$772.12** (rounded) documentary stamp tax

$617.70 + $772.12 = **$1,389.82** transfer taxes

CHAPTER

5

COMPUTING MONTHLY PAYMENTS: PRINCIPAL, INTEREST, TAXES, AND INSURANCE

▶ *Before You Begin, You Need to Know . . .*

mill = $\frac{1}{1,000}$ of \$1, or $\frac{1}{10}$ of a cent, or .001

Rules of thumb:

PMI = $\frac{1}{2}$ of 1% = .005

Hazard = $\frac{1}{2}$ of 1% = .005

PROPERTY TAXES

A number of factors—including the intended use of the property (i.e., commercial, industrial, or residential), the value of the property, and the tax rate (often expressed in mills)—go into determining property taxes. State, municipal, county, town, school district, and other local agencies such as water and sewer authorities may also levy property taxes. The money raised is used to pay for services, such as schools, fire and police protection, parks, libraries and other facilities and services.

▶ *Tip*

Communities determine millage rates by taking their total budget requirement and subtracting all revenues from sources other than property taxes. What remains represents the amount the community needs to collect from property taxes.

Taxing authorities determine the value of the property in a variety of ways, among them the property's assessed value, its actual market value, or its estimated market value. The local tax assessor, a government employee whose job is similar that of a home appraiser, generally determines the value of the property.

▶ *Tip*

Property taxes are usually deductible from federal income tax returns.

Calculating Taxable Value

The principle elements of the property tax consist of the tax rate and the tax base. Although the method varies from place to place, in general the tax base is determined by appraising the value of property according to statutory requirements to find the "taxable value." The result is multiplied by the level of assessment to get the assessed value; the tax rate is then applied to the assessed value to determine the total amount of taxes due. The formula is:

taxable value × level of assessment = assessed value

assessed value × tax rate = total property tax

The level of assessment, known as the "rate of assessment," is generally expressed as a ratio of assessed value to taxable value. Again, in some places, assessments are at full value; in others it can be a percentage of full value. The formula is:

taxable value × level of assessment = assessed value

Taxable Value Example:

If the taxable value of a single-family residence is $200,000, and the level of assessment is 35%, then the assessed value would be:

$200,000 (taxable value) × .35 (level of assessment) = $70,000 (assessed value)

If the tax rate is 627 mills or .627 per $1,000 of assessed valuation, to get the total amount of property taxes for a year, divide:

$70,000 ÷ $1,000 = $70

Then, multiply.

$70 × .627 = $4,389 property tax due

▶ *Tip*

Most communities have a separate property tax for schools; in some places, a homeowner may pay a village, town, and/or county tax. When calculating the total amount of property taxes on any piece of property, make sure to add the various taxes.

PUT YOUR TAXABLE VALUE CALCULATION SKILLS TO WORK

1. The taxes on a farm in Franklin Township are 32 mills per $1 of assessed valuation for the town and 19 mills for the school district. Assessed valuation is $165,000. What are the annual taxes on this property?

2. A home sold for $1.5 million dollars. Determine the assessed value taxable value if the rate of assessment is 25%.

3. On the home in question 2, calculate each of the following tax rates: city 5.3 mills, county 7.6 mills, and school district 6.5 mills. Then, calculate the total property tax on this home.

Caps on Property Tax Rates

Some states have outright limits on the property tax rate; for example, $.05 per $1.00 of assessed value ($5 per $100 of assessed value).

Other states have homestead exemptions or exemptions for those older than age 65 or for the disabled. They remove part of a home's value from taxation in order to lower taxes. These exemptions usually apply only to primary residences; they may not be used by corporations or for investment properties. Sometimes, an owner may qualify for more than one exemption; other times the owner may have to choose the most advantageous one.

Sometimes, rebates are based solely on income, for example:

Gross Income	Rebate Amount (% of Property Tax)
$100,000 or less	20% (maximum $2,000)
$100,001 to $150,000	15% (maximum $1,500)
$150,001 and $250,000	10% (maximum $1,000)

Figure 5.1 Rebate

Still other states have homeowner rebates based on a percentage of gross income and amount of taxes paid, for example:

Gross Income	Rebate Amount (% of Property Tax)
Not more than $70,000	$1,000 to $1,200
$70,001 to $125,000	$600 to $800
$125,001 to $200,000	$500

Figure 5.2 Rebate

In such cases, use the following formula to determine the amount of the rebate:

property taxes paid – % of gross income = rebate

Limits of various kinds are usually placed on rebates. In this case:

- the rebate amount is equal to property taxes paid minus 5% of gross income, but never less than the lower rebate amount
- no rebate on incomes over $200,000
- the amount of rebate is limited to the maximum rebate amount for the homeowner's income level
- the amount of rebate may never be more than the amount of property taxes actually paid

Caps Example:

Assume the tax on a piece of property is $4,100.72. There is a cap of $5 per $100 of assessed valuation, which is $85,000. To find out whether the tax qualifies for a reduction in taxes, use the formula:

$$\frac{4,100.72}{85,000 \div 100} = \frac{4,100.72}{850}$$

$$4,100.72 \div 850 = \$4.82$$

The taxes due are below the $5 cap.

Exemptions Example:

Now, let's assume the home was originally assessed at $100,000, but the owner qualified for a 15% exemption.

$100,000 × .15 = $85,000

The owner will pay taxes based on the home as if it were worth only $85,000.

Rebates Example:

Assuming the percentage of gross income is 5%, use the rebate formula shown here:

property taxes paid – % of gross income = rebate

and Figure 5.2 to determine the amount of rebate. Assume this homeowner has a gross income of $75,500. We can determine that the homeowner qualifies for a rebate. To determine the amount of the rebate:

$4,172 – ($75,500 × .05) = rebate

$4,172 – $3,775 = $397

Because this is less than the lower rebate amount for an income of $75,500, the homeowner would receive $600.

Using Figure 5.1, the calculation would be:

$4,172 × .2 = $834.40

PUT YOUR CAPS, EXEMPTIONS, AND REBATE CALCULATION SKILLS TO WORK

4. Assume a cap of $7.50 for every $100 in assessed valuation. A property is assessed at $432,500, and the total property tax rate is .082. How much tax is due on this property?

5. The state offers a homeowners exemption of $15,000; the home's assessed value is $332,025. The total tax rate is 17.5 mills. Calculate the total property tax.

6. Using Figure 5.1, calculate the rebate if the owner's gross income is $225,000 and the total property tax paid is $6,742.53.

7. Using Figure 5.2, calculate the rebate if the owner's gross income is $275,000 and the total property tax paid is $7,373.

Use the following information to answer questions 8–11. A home's assessed evaluation is $425,000. There is a homestead exemption of $22,500.

8. Calculate the taxable value.

9. Calculate the total property taxes if the rate is .0072.

10. How much did the exemption save the homeowner?

11. If the owner's income is $99,500, using Figure 5.2, determine the amount of his rebate if the percentage of gross income is 2.5% and none of the other rules apply.

INSURANCE

So far we've covered the computations that go into mortgage calculations and payments, the transfer taxes that may be associated with the purchase of property, as well as the various property taxes. The last leg of the equation is insurance—which includes private mortgage insurance (if required by the lender) and homeowners and hazard insurance.

Private Mortgage Insurance (PMI)

As a rule, lenders require PMI on all mortgages when the down payment is less than 20%, and although things are changing, PMI still is required on jumbo mortgages. According to the Mortgage Bankers Association of America, PMI charges vary depending on the size of the down payment and the loan, but they typically amount to about $\frac{1}{2}$ of 1% of the loan, although the amount may be reduced in later years. Beyond 20 years, the monthly PMI premium changes to $\frac{0.2\%}{12}$ of the initial mortgage amount, regardless of the size of the down payment.

In some cases, PMI for the first year is paid upfront at closing; in others, PMI is included in monthly mortgage payments from the beginning. In this case, the insurer normally collects an escrow equal to two months' premium at the beginning of the mortgage.

By law, PMI is paid until the loan-to-value (LTV) ratio falls to 78%, and the homeowner may request that it cease when the LTV falls to below 80% of the original loan. Appreciation does not factor into PMI; it is based on the original loan.

▶ *Tip*

Mortgage insurance premiums are not tax deductible.

Hazard Insurance

In some locations, the lender will require hazard insurance to cover property damage caused by natural disasters, such as fire, wind, and storms. Earthquakes and floods are not always covered by hazard insurance, and insurance for these may have to be purchased separately.

Premiums for hazard insurance are based on the appraised value of the property, the age of the building, construction methods, and known natural hazards in the area. As with PMI, the borrower may have to pay for first year of hazard insurance at the closing; in other circumstances, hazard insurance is included in monthly mortgage payments from the beginning. Here again the insurer normally collects an escrow equal to two months' premium at the beginning of the mortgage.

▶ *Tip*

Homeowners insurance covers a dwelling, its contents, as well as personal liability. Hazard insurance may be included in some homeowners policies, but not all. Depending on where the property is located, some buyers may choose to purchase hazard insurance and/or flood and earthquake protection.

PMI and Hazard Insurance Example:

The selling price of a home is $163,000; the mortgage is $138,550, or 15%. The monthly mortgage is $853.08 at 6.25%. Assuming the annual PMI is $\frac{1}{2}$ of 1%, the additional cost with PMI is calculated as follows:

$138,550 (amount of mortgage) × .005 (PMI) = $692.75

To calculate the monthly charge, divide:

$692.75 ÷ 12 = $57.729 = $57.73

To get the total monthly payment, add:

$853.08 + $57.73 = $910.81

The identical calculation is used for hazard insurance.

▶ *Tip*

If both are to be included in the mortgage payment, simplify the equation by multiplying by .01 and then by dividing by 12.

PUT YOUR INSURANCE CALCULATION SKILLS TO WORK

12. Assume a monthly mortgage payment of $1,752.62 on a 30-year $295,700 mortgage. Calculate the annual payment inclusive of PMI and hazard insurance.

13. Assume a monthly mortgage payment of $2,330.92 on a 20-year $332,000 mortgage. Calculate the monthly charge for PMI. Assuming no hazard insurance is required, what is the monthly payment?

14. On a jumbo mortgage of $800,000 where the buyer is putting 15% down, the monthly mortgage payment at 6.6% is $5,109.27. Calculate the charge for PMI. Assuming no hazard insurance is required, what is the monthly payment?

15. Assume instead that the buyer in question 2 puts 20% down; the mortgage amount would be $752,940, and at the same interest rate, the monthly payment would be $4,808.72. Instead of mortgage insurance, the buyer decides to take a second mortgage on the difference ($47,060) and negotiates a rate of 6.4% so that mortgage comes to $294.36. Exclusive of other costs, would the buyer reduce her monthly payments? If so, by how much?

CALCULATING PITI

Principal, interest, taxes, and insurance (PITI) combine to equal the total monthly costs associated with a mortgage.

In Chapters 3 and 4, we covered all the factors that go into calculating loans, mortgages, and interest payments:

- type of mortgage: fixed rate, adjustable rate, conventional, FHA, and others
- minimum down payment required
- loan term (length of loan)
- contract interest rate
- points (may also be called loan discount points) and origination fees

In this chapter, we examined the impact of:

- taxes
- insurance
- private mortgage insurance (PMI) premiums and hazard insurance

PITI Example:

For the purposes of calculating PITI, it is not necessary to know what portion of a mortgage payment is principal and what portion is interest; therefore, the formula is:

mortgage payment (principal + interest) + taxes + insurance = PITI

PUT YOUR TAXABLE VALUE CALCULATION SKILLS TO WORK

16. Assuming a monthly mortgage payment of $764.88 per month, total property taxes of $4,122.43 per year, and hazard insurance payments of $637.50 per year, calculate the monthly PITI.

ANSWERS

Answers appear in **boldface**.

1. 32 mills = .032
   19 mills = .019
   .032 + .019 = .051
   $165,000 (assessed value) × .051 = **$8,415** annual taxes

2. $1,500,000 × .75 = **$1,125,000** taxable value

3. 5.3 mills = .0053
   7.6 mills = .0076
   6.5 mills = .0065
   $1,125,000 × .0053 = $5,962.50 city
   $1,125,000 × .0065 = $7,312.50 county
   $1,125,000 × .0076 = $8,550 school district
   $5,962.50 + $8,550 + $7,323.50= **$21,836** total property tax

4. $432,500 (assessed value) ÷ 100 = 4,325 hundreds
   $7.50 × $4,325 = $32,437.50
   $432,500 × .082 = $35,465
   $32,437.50 property tax owed

5. $332,025 (assessed value) − $15,000 (homestead exemption) = $317,025
   (taxable value)
   17.5 mills = .0175
   $317,025 × .0175 = **$5,547.94** (rounded) property tax

6. $6,742.53 × .1 = **$674.25** rebate

7. **No rebate due.** The owner's gross income exceeds the maximum of
   $200,000.

8. $425,000 − $22,500 = **$402,500** taxable value

9. $402,500 × .0072 = **$2,898** total property taxes

10. $22,500 × .0072 = **$162** saved

11. $2,898 (property tax) − (.025 × $99,500) (percent of gross income) = rebate
$2,898 − 2,487.50 = **$410.50** rebate

12. $295,700 (total mortgage) × .01 (PMI and hazard insurance) = **$2,957** total annual payment

13. $332,000 (total mortgage) × .005 (annual PMI) = $\frac{\$1,660}{12}$ (monthly PMI)
$3,160 (PMI) ÷ 12 = $138.33 monthly PMI
$2,390.92 (monthly mortgage) + $138.33 = **$2,529.25** monthly payment

14. $800,000 (total mortgage) × .005 (annual PMI) = $\frac{\$4,000}{12}$ (monthly PMI)
$4,000 (PMI) ÷ 12 = 333.33 (monthly PMI)
$5,109.27 (monthly mortgage) + 333.33 = **$5,442.60** monthly payment

15. Yes.
$4,802.72 (monthly payment first mortgage) + $294.36 (monthly payment second mortgage) = $5,097.08
$5,442.60 (monthly payment on $800,000 mortgage including PMI) − 5,097.08 = **$345.52** monthly payment reduction

16. $764.88 (monthly mortgage) + $\frac{\$4,122.32}{12}$ (monthly taxes) + $\frac{\$637.50}{12}$ monthly insurance) = total monthly PITI
$4,122.32 ÷ 12 = $343.53
$637.50 ÷ 12 = $53.13
$764.88 + 343.53 + 53.13 = **$1,161.54** PITI

PART

III

APPRAISING REAL ESTATE

CHAPTER

LAND AND AREA CALCULATIONS

 ### *Before You Begin, You Need to Know . . .*

12 inches = 1 foot	640 acres = 1 square mile
144 square inches = 1 square foot	township = square, 6 miles by 6 miles or 36 square miles
3 feet = 1 yard	section = square, 1 mile by 1 mile
5,280 feet = 1 mile	circle = 360 degrees (360°) or 4 quadrants of 90°
1,760 yards = 1 mile	1 degree (1°) = 60 minutes (60′)
43,560 square feet = 1 acre	1 minute (1′) = 60 seconds (60″)

HOW TO CALCULATE THE AREA OF ANYTHING

Finding area is one of the most frequently performed calculations in real estate. Determining the square footage of a piece of land, house, condominium, or room will require area calculations. Whatever the unit of measure—feet, acres, yards, or miles—you need to know how to perform the calculations. Generally, it's a simple case of multiplication.

$$\text{length} \times \text{width} = \text{area of square or rectangle}$$
$$\tfrac{1}{2}(\text{base} \times \text{height}) = \text{area of a triangle}$$
$$\pi r^2 = \text{area of a circle } (3.14 \approx \pi)$$

Rectangle Example:

To determine the gross square footage of a condo that is 60 feet long by 25 feet wide, multiply:

$$60 \times 25 = 1{,}500 \text{ square feet}$$

▶ *Tip*

Gross square footage is total square footage. This is not the same as net square footage or usable square footage.

a plot of land 3 acres × 5 acres = 15 square acres
If you wanted to know how many square feet were in 15 acres, you would multiply

$15 \times 43{,}560$ (the number of square feet in 1 acre) = 653,400 square feet

If this same property was on the market for $1,100,000, you could determine the price per square foot as well as the price per acre. The formula is:

sale price per square feet (or square acre) = price per square foot (or square acre)

$1,100,000 ÷ 653,400 square feet = $1.68 per square foot

$1,100,000 ÷ 15 acres = $73,333.33 per acre

Note: In each case, the answer is rounded to the nearest cent.

Triangle Example:

The base of a triangular-shaped center island on a road is 450 feet, and the height is 100 feet. The property is selling for $1.50 per square foot.

$(.5 \times 450) \times 100 =$ square footage

$225 \times 100 = 22,500$ square feet

$22,500 \times \$1.50 = \$33,750$

Circle Example:

There aren't many circular pieces of property, buildings, or rooms, but occasionally, you do come across one. Let's say you find an antique carousel house for sale, and its radius is 40 feet. The asking price is $200,000.

$(3.14 \times 40^2) =$ square footage

$3.14 \times 1,600 = 5,024$ square feet

$\$200,000 \div 5,024 = \$39.81$ per square foot

▶ ***Tip***

If a property is irregularly shaped, divide it into its component parts, calculate area, and then add the results.

PUT YOUR AREA CALCULATION SKILLS TO WORK

1. How many acres are there in 102,000 square feet?

2. A 2,200 square foot condo is listed at $450,000. How much per square foot is it selling for?

3. Assume an L-shaped lot is composed of a square 1,200 × 1,200 and a rectangle 400 × 600. What is the total square footage?

4. Convert the answer to question 3 into acres. Reminder: 1 acre = 43,560 square feet. This is a percentage problem.

METHODS USED TO DESCRIBE REAL ESTATE

There are three methods used to describe real estate: lot and block, metes and bounds, and the U.S. government survey system (also called the U.S. rectangular survey system). The **lot and block method** requires practically no math because boundary lines, streets, actual measurements, and easements are included on a plat map, which is publicly recorded.

Metes and Bounds

The **metes and bounds method** yields the least accurate form of legal description. Metes refers to the length or measurement (for example, feet or miles) of the parcel; bounds refers to its boundaries, and is expressed in terms of direction and degrees on a compass.

A compass has four primary directions: north (N), east (E), south (S), and west (W), which can be illustrated as follows:

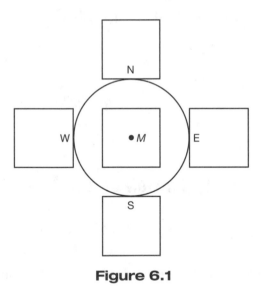

Figure 6.1

When measuring metes and bounds, start from the center. According to *Real Estate Math, Sixth Edition* (Dearborn 2005, 45), "the point of beginning (POB) and all turning points should be regarded as the exact center of a circle." The center is usually an existing monument (for example, a gazebo) or marker set precisely by a surveyor (shown as • *M* in Figure 6.1). To describe a parcel using the metes and bounds method, use north or south as your starting point. For example, "In metes and bounds legal descriptions, all directions begin with a reference to either north or south—the primary indicators" (Dearborn 2005, 45). Then, measure the distance in all directions. The result is expressed in terms of the number of degrees, the distance, and the direction.

Metes and Bounds Example:

Beginning at the monument, head north 30° 82.5' east and south 42° 102' 00" west. (See Figure 6.2. The solid line indicates the first direction, the dotted line the second.)

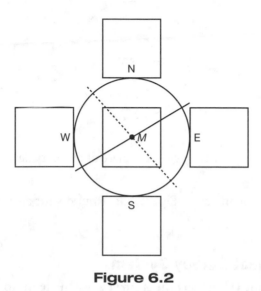

Figure 6.2

Although you will probably never have to write the metes and bounds of a parcel, it is important to understand what they mean so that, if necessary, you can walk the property line. Some descriptions are long, especially if the property is irregular in form, but they all follow the same principle and sound something like this:

Beginning at the intersection on the southwest corner of State Street, head west 200 feet, then north at a 90° angle onto Elm Street for 50 feet, then east into Schubert Alley 200 feet, then south 50 feet, and then back to the point of beginning in a straight line.

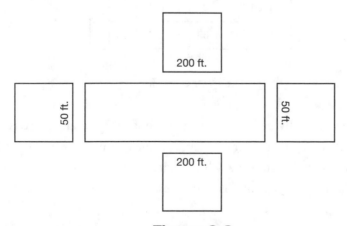

Figure 6.3

PUT YOUR METES AND BOUNDS SKILLS TO WORK

5. Draw a line in the circle demonstrating a boundary running north 40° west.

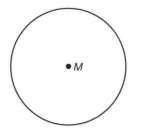

6. What is the square footage of the piece of property described in Figure 6.3?

7. What part of an acre is Figure 6.3? (Round your answer to two decimal points.)

U.S. Government Survey System

The last method, the **U.S. government survey system,** tends to be used mostly in western states and is not used in every state. It is based on a grid of numbered squares (6 miles by 6 miles) representing townships; each township contains 36 sections, each 1 mile by 1 mile (see Figure 6.4), or 640 acres.

North 6 miles

6	5	4	3	2	1
7	8	9	10	11	12
18	17	16	15	14	13
24	23	22	21	20	19
30	29	28	27	26	25
31	32	33	34	35	36

West 6 miles   East 6 miles

South 6 miles

Figure 6.4

These are usually divided into smaller and smaller rectangles. This is done by dividing each section—no matter how large or small—into quarters. A quadrangle is four townships high by four townships wide, or 24 miles square. Each standard 1-mile-by-1-mile section contains 640 acres. Fractional sections may contain more or less than 640 acres.

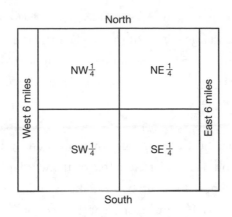

Figure 6.5

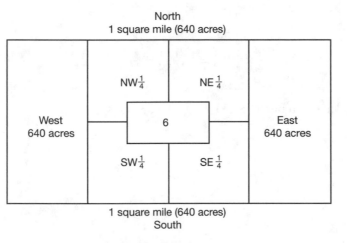

Figure 6.6

PUT YOUR GOVERNMENT SURVEY SKILLS TO WORK

8. Using Figure 6.6, locate the southeast corner, and subdivide it into quarters.

9. How large is each quarter in the southeast corner in miles? Section 6 measures 1 mile by 1 mile or 1 square mile.

▶ *Tip*

To determine the size of one of the new parcels in miles, you need to determine what $\frac{1}{4}$ of $\frac{1}{4}$ of the southeast $\frac{1}{4}$ is.

10. Assume now that the northeast of the southeast corner is divided into quarters. How large is each of the newly formed quarters in acres? Section 6 measures 640 acres, or one square mile. To determine the size of the northeast $\frac{1}{4}$ of $\frac{1}{4}$ of the southeast $\frac{1}{4}$, set up the following equation: $640 \times \frac{1}{4} \times \frac{1}{4} \times \frac{1}{4} = x$

Often we must calculate the area of more than one parcel; these calculations are more complicated. You will be alerted to this by the word *and* in the description. It means that you will have to set up two equations and add the results. Suppose a parcel is described: north $\frac{2}{3}$, northeast $\frac{1}{4}$, south $\frac{1}{2}$ section 27, *and* south $\frac{1}{2}$, southwest $\frac{1}{4}$, north $\frac{1}{2}$ section 26. To determine the combined acreage:

$$\text{Section } 27 = \frac{2}{3} \times \frac{1}{4} \times \frac{1}{2} = \frac{2 \times 1 \times 1}{3 \times 4 \times 2} = \frac{2}{24} = \frac{1}{12}$$

$$\frac{640}{12} = 53.33 \text{ acres}$$

$$\text{Section } 26 = \frac{1}{2} \times \frac{1}{4} \times \frac{1}{2} = \frac{1 \times 1 \times 1}{2 \times 4 \times 2} = \frac{1}{16}$$

$$\frac{640}{16} = 40 \text{ acres}$$

Total acres in parcel 53.33 + 40 = 93.33 acres

ANSWERS

Answers appear in **boldface**.

1. $102{,}000 \div 43{,}560 = $ **2.34** (rounded)

2. $\$450{,}000 \div 2{,}200 = $ **$204.55** (rounded)

3. $(1{,}200 \times 1{,}200) + (400 \times 600) =$
$1{,}440{,}000 + 240{,}000 = $ **1,680,000** square feet

4. $1{,}680{,}000 \div 43{,}560 = $ **38.57** (rounded)

5. Starting from the center of the circle • M, head directly toward the top of the circle (north), then travel to the left (west), just a bit less than halfway.

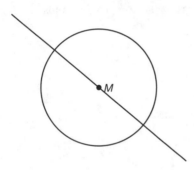

6. $200 \times 50 = $ **10,000** square feet

7. $\frac{10{,}000}{43{,}560} = \frac{x}{100}$
$43{,}560x = 1{,}000{,}000$
$x = $ **22.96%**

8. Your answer should look like this:

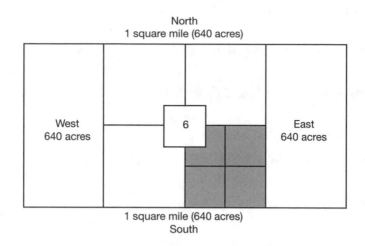

North
1 square mile (640 acres)

West
640 acres

6

East
640 acres

1 square mile (640 acres)
South

9. $1 \times \frac{1}{4} \times \frac{1}{4} = \frac{1}{16}$ mile

Alternatively, you could convert the fractions to decimals, $\frac{1}{4} = .25$

$1 \times .25 \times .25 = .0625$ square miles

10. $640 \times \frac{1}{4} \times \frac{1}{4} \times \frac{1}{4} = x$

$4 \times 4 \times 4 = 64$

$\frac{640}{64} = 10$ acres

7

MARKET VALUE OF RESIDENTIAL PROPERTIES

In the home real estate market, a common definition of market value is the price a particular house, in "as is" condition, will sell for within 30 to 90 days of the date of appraisal.

From an investment point of view, one estimate of market value is the price the property would command based on the "highest and best use" to which it can be put. This is not necessarily the way it is being used at the time of the appraisal, but rather its highest *potential* value. To make this assessment, an appraiser determines:

- what uses are legally allowed
- which of these are physically possible
- which of these are financially feasible
- which one is maximally productive for the site

In making the appraisal, it is assumed that the buyer will put the property to that use. Following are three approaches commonly used to appraise real estate:

1. cost
2. sales comparison
3. income capitalization

CALCULATING MARKET VALUE USING THE COST APPROACH

To estimate the value of a property using this method, use the formula:

land value + depreciated value of any improvements = value

Depreciation is any loss in value that results from physical deterioration, functional, or external obsolescence. **Accrued depreciation** is the amount of depreciation that has accumulated since initial construction, or the difference between the current appraised value and the cost to replace the building altogether.

Often, the cost approach is combined with the sales comparison approach, in particular, to estimate the cost of the land and depreciation. For example, new home construction costs can be determined by adding the labor, material, and so on; land values and depreciation are best determined by analyzing comparable data.

▶ *Tip*

The cost approach is most reliable when applied to newer buildings and special use commercial properties, such as a theater.

Replacement Cost

To estimate the value of improvements, use one of two formulas:

reproduction cost new – depreciation = value of improvements

where **reproduction cost** is the cost of reproducing an exact replica.

Or

replacement cost new – depreciation = value of improvements

where **replacement cost** is the cost of building a house or commercial property of the same utility, using contemporary techniques and materials. In practice, most appraisals use replacement cost rather than reproduction cost.

Appraisers generally begin with a scope of work to define their assignment. Depending on the approach, activities could include an analysis of cost per square foot, first in total and then room by room. The cost per square foot of an unfinished attic or basement is quite different from the cost of a fully equipped high-end kitchen or bath. Prices vary in different parts of the country, so appraisals are based on local cost. A number of publications are available to help appraisers determine what values should be used for each part of the house as well as for other structures on the property, for example, an unattached garage or a barn.

The appraiser next assesses the unique qualities, if any, of the structure—for example, high ceilings, moldings, and internal amenities such as fireplaces. Outside landscaping, pools, patios, and so on are evaluated in residential property. Similar steps are used in appraising agricultural land; for example, a fenced pasture would be taken into account.

> *Replacement Cost Example:*
> Let's assume the following square footage and costs to determine the replacement value of a home:
>
> | | |
> |---|---|
> | living areas: 1,581 square feet at $100/sq. ft. | = $158,100 |
> | attached garage: 400 square feet at $50/sq. ft. | = $20,000 |
> | total value of dwelling | = $178,100 |

PUT YOUR REPLACEMENT COST CALCULATION SKILLS TO WORK

1. Replacement costs on a home are estimated as follows: a recently remodeled kitchen and bathroom, 17' × 15' at $150/sq. ft.; remaining living space, 25' × 60' at $95/sq. ft.; an unattached garage, 20' × 22' at $45/sq. ft.; and a wraparound porch, 10' × 50' at $22.50/sq. ft. What is the replacement cost?

Depreciation

There are two methods used in real estate for estimating depreciation. One is the **straight-line depreciation method**, which spreads the total depreciation over a building's estimated **economic life** (how much longer the building can be used productively). Appraisers base their analysis of economic life on a combination of experience and comparison with similar structures of similar age.

The other is the **age-life depreciation method**. Here, depreciation is determined by comparing a building's economic life to its **effective age**. This method is considered more accurate because it takes the actual condition of the property into account rather than its chronological age only.

► *Tip*

The way in which a building has been maintained and/or improved can add or subtract years from its effective age. Neither economic age nor effective age is the same as chronological age.

Straight-Line Depreciation Method

To calculate the effect of depreciation on market value using the straight-line depreciation method, use the formula:

replacement cost new ÷ years of economic life = depreciation per year × age of structure = accrued depreciation

Straight-line Depreciation Example:

Assume that the total replacement cost of a dwelling is $190,000 and that the home is five years old. It has an estimated economic life of 50 years. Plugging these numbers into the formula for determining accrued depreciation using the straight-line depreciation method, we get:

$190,000 (replacement cost new) ÷ 50 (years of economic life) = $3,800 (depreciation per year) × 5 (age of structure) = $19,000 (accrued depreciation)

PUT YOUR STRAIGHT-LINE DEPRECIATION CALCULATION SKILLS TO WORK

2. The replacement cost of a 12-year-old beach house is $625,000; its estimated economic life is 62 years. What is the accrued depreciation?

Age-Life Depreciation Method

The second method, age-life depreciation, determines accrued depreciation using the formula:

(effective age ÷ economic life) × replacement cost = age-life accrued depreciation

Age-Life Depreciation Example:

Take the same scenario we used in the straight-line example: The total replacement cost of a dwelling is $190,000, and the home is five years old. It has an estimated economic life of 50 years. This time, factor in the building's effective age of seven.

[7 (effective age) ÷ 50 (economic life)] = .14 (age-life accrued depreciation) × $190,000 (replacement cost) = $26,600 (accrued depreciation)

PUT YOUR AGE-LIFE DEPRECIATION CALCULATION SKILLS TO WORK

3. Now let's take that same 12-year-old beach house: Replacement cost is $625,000; its estimated economic life is 62 years, and its effective age is 10. What is the accrued depreciation?

Using Percentages in Depreciation Problems

To express the annual rate of depreciation as a percentage, use the formula:

annual depreciation rate = 100% ÷ years of economic life

The years of economic life can be determined with the formula:

years of economic life = 100% ÷ annual depreciation rate

Depreciation Percentage Examples:

Use the earlier example:

$190,000 (replacement cost new) ÷ 50 (years of economic life) = $3,800 (depreciation per year) × 5 (age of structure) = $19,000 (accrued depreciation)

To determine the rate of accrued depreciation in this example:

$x = 100\% \div 50$

$x = 2\%$ rate of accrued depreciation

Similarly, you can derive the economic life of a property, if you know the rate of accrued depreciation.

years of economic life × 2% = 100%

100% ÷ 2% = 50 years of economic life

PUT YOUR DEPRECIATION PERCENTAGE CALCULATION SKILLS TO WORK

4. If a building has an annual depreciation rate of 3.2%, what is its economic life?

5. If the building in question 4 is five years old, what is its rate of accrued depreciation?

6. If a dwelling's economic life is 60 years, what is its annual accrued depreciation rate?

7. If the replacement value of the dwelling in question 6 is $132,500 and the dwelling is seven years old, what is its accrued depreciation expressed in dollars?

Land Value

Land value is what the property would sell for if it were vacant. The easiest way to obtain the value is through recent sales of comparable vacant lots. If no vacant lots are available, an appraiser can determine the value by:

- obtaining selling prices of houses in the same neighborhood on similarly sized lots with similar characteristics
- estimating the replacement cost of the improvements
- deducting depreciation from the replacement cost
- deducting the depreciated cost of the improvements from the selling price of the property. The difference is the approximate value of the land.

The formula for arriving at the value of the comparable property is:
replacement cost – accrued depreciation = depreciated value of building
selling price – depreciated value of building = selling price of comparable vacant land ÷ lot size = price per square foot × lot size of subject property = value of actual property's land

Land Value Example:
The comparable property is on a 6,000-square-foot lot and sold for $83,000. The replacement value of the building is estimated at $61,000; the accrued depreciation is estimated at $20,000. The actual property is on a 6,500-square-foot lot.
$61,000 (replacement cost) – $20,000 (accrued depreciation) = $41,000 (depreciated value of building)
$83,000 (selling price) – $41,000 (depreciated value of building) = $42,000
$42,000 (selling price of vacant land) ÷ 6,000 sq. ft. (lot size) = $7.00/sq. ft. (value of land/sq. ft.)
$7 (price/sq. ft.) × 6,500 sq. ft. (lot size of actual property) = $45,500 (value of subject property's land)

▶ *Tip*

The most accurate appraisal would be an actual plot plan with lot dimensions and improvements drawn to scale together with pictures of the site, as well as neighboring street and lot improvements.

PUT YOUR LAND VALUE CALCULATION SKILLS TO WORK

8. The comparable property is on two acres and sold for $2.25 million. The estimated replacement value of the building is $1.75 million; the accrued depreciation is estimated at $200,000. The actual property is on a 3.5-acre lot.

CALCULATING MARKET VALUE USING SALES COMPARISON APPROACH

As we've seen in looking at land value, the sales comparison approach is based on the price of similar properties—comparables—ideally those that have sold recently. The properties chosen are as similar as possible to the one being appraised, and adjustments are made to account for differences. If there are a sufficient number of comparable sales, the sales comparison approach is quite reliable in getting to the real value of the subject property in a given market.

In addition to selling price, square footage, extra bathrooms, hardwood floors, fireplaces, views, and curb appeal (among other factors) affect the price of a property and are considered when determining an accurate appraisal of a property's value. In addition to examining the dwelling and the property itself, appraisers familiarize themselves with the value of certain features and use this information to determine value. These calculations can cause the appraisal price of the subject property to increase or decrease.

The math involved in assessing comparables is simple arithmetic—adding and subtracting to adjust for differences among properties, multiplying to determine such things as square footage, lot size, etc., and dividing to determine average prices.

Comparable Example:
Assume that the subject property is a 15-year-old, four-bedroom, $3\frac{1}{2}$-bath, 2,750-square-foot, two-story colonial on a quiet cul-de-sac in a residential neighborhood. It has an attached two-car garage. A comparable property has a nicely finished walk-out basement with a bedroom, its own bath, and a patio. The comparable

property is on a corner lot of a busy thoroughfare. The comparable property sold a month earlier for $527,500.

Differences between the two properties:

Comparable Property	Subject Property	+/– Value
Patio	No patio	– $2,500
Finished walk-out basement	No basement	– $79,000
Three bathrooms	Two bathrooms	– $5,000
Corner lot, busy thoroughfare	Quiet cul-de-sac	+ $2,500
Selling price comparable	**Selling price subject**	**– $84,000**

To derive the estimated market value, adjust for the differences between the two houses, and add or subtract from the selling price of the comparable to determine the value of the subject property.

$527,500 – $84,000 = $443,500

PUT YOUR SALES COMPARISON CALCULATION SKILLS TO WORK

Comparable Property	+/– Value	Subject Property	+/– Value
none		Oversized wooden deck with planters	$7,500
Landscaped pool and stone barbecue		none	($22,000)
none		Large new master bathroom	$20,000
3,000 square feet		2,700 square feet	($30,000)
Powder room ($\frac{1}{2}$ bath)		None	($2,500)
Total +/–			
Selling price comparable	**$331,750**	**Selling price subject**	

9. Using the above table, calculate the +/– value of the subject home and estimated market value.

10. Assume that three comparable properties have sold for $127,500; $139,800; and $131,750. There is no discernible difference in the properties. What is the estimated market value of the subject property?

ANSWERS

Answers appear in **boldface**.

1. 17' × 15' = 255 sq. ft. × $150 = $38,250
    25' × 60' = 1,500 sq. ft. × $95 = $142,500
    20' × 22' = 440 sq. ft. × $45 = $19,800
    10' × 50' = 500 sq. ft. × $22.50 = $11,250
    $38,250 + $142,500 + $19,800 + $11,250 = **$211,800** replacement cost

2. $625,000 (replacement cost new) ÷ 62 (years of economic life) = $10,080.65 (depreciation per year) $10,080.65 × 12 (age of structure) = **$120,967.74** accrued depreciation

3. [10 (effective age) ÷ 62 (economic life)] = .1613 (age-life accrued depreciation × $625,000 (replacement cost) = **$100,806.45** accrued depreciation

4. 100% ÷ 3.2% (annual depreciation rate) = **31.25** years of economic life

5. 5 years × 3.2% = **16%** accrued depreciation

6. 100% ÷ 60 (years of economic life) = **1.6667%** (rounded) annual accrued depreciation rate

7. 1.67% (annual depreciation rate) × 7 years = 11.67% accrued depreciation
    $132,500 × 11.67% = **$15,458.33** accrued depreciation

8. $1,750,000 (replacement cost) − $200,000 (accrued depreciation) = $1,550,000 (depreciated value of building)
    $2,250,000 (selling price) − $1,550,000 (depreciated value of building) = $700,000
    $700,000 (selling price of vacant land) ÷ 2 acres (size of comparable property) = value of land per acre
    $350,000 (price per acre) × 3.5 acres (size of actual property) = **$1,225,000** value of actual property's land

9. $331,750 (selling price/comparable) − ($22,000 + $2,500) + ($7,500 + $20,000 − $30,000)
    $331,750 − $24,500 − $2,500 = **$304,750** selling price subject

10. ($127,500 + $139,800 + $131,750) ÷ 3 = $399,050 ÷ 3 = **$133,017**

CHAPTER

MARKET VALUE OF INVESTMENT PROPERTIES

Three main methods are used to calculate the value of investment properties: direct or income capitalization, discounted cash flow, and gross income multiplier. A commercial appraisal typically values a property based on income, replacement cost, and sales comparison.

CALCULATING MARKET VALUE USING INCOME (DIRECT) CAPITALIZATION APPROACH

Using this approach, the amount of income a property produces is used to project the current value of those revenues into the future. This method requires dividing the annual net operating income (NOI) by the appropriate capitalization (CAP) rate, also known as overall rate of return.

NOI ÷ CAP rate = estimated market value

Net Operating Income

To calculate NOI:

STEP 1: Start by figuring out what the property's effective gross income (EGI) is by using the formula:

potential gross income (PGI) × vacancy and collection loss (VCL) = EGI

PGI is the income from property if fully rented and all rents are collected. The formula is:

units × annual rent per unit = PGI

VCL is the total of uncollected rents either resulting from bad debts or unrented units.

STEP 2: Add up the operating expenses (OE)—for example, management, legal, and accounting fees, insurance, maintenance, supplies, taxes, utilities, garbage, etc.

STEP 3: Subtract the operating expenses from the EGI to arrive at the net operating income:

EGI – OE = NOI

Or, consolidate the steps, using the following equation:

PGI – VCL – OE = NOI

Net Operating Income Example:

To determine the NOI of a property where PGI = $102,000, VCL = $27,500 and OE = $33,000:

$102,000 (PGI) – $27,500 (VCL) – $33,000 (OE) = $41,500 (NOI)

If you know any three parts of this equation, you can calculate the fourth. For example, you can determine the PGI if you know that the NOI is $163,560, VCL is $37,618, and OE is $29,800. The formula is:

NOI + VCL + OE = PGI

$163,560 + $37,618 + $29,800 = $230,978

You can also calculate the percentage of any part. Using the previous example, what percentage of PGI is NOI?

$163,560 ÷ $230,978 = .708 = 71%

PUT YOUR NET OPERATING INCOME CALCULATION SKILLS TO WORK

1. The projected gross income of a building is $83,046. The property has a vacancy, and the collection rate is 15%. Calculate the effective gross income. The operating expense is $22,330.

2. What is the net operating income?

3. The NOI of an office building is $1,236,792. If the effective gross income is $1,650,000, how much are the operating expenses?

4. What percentage of EGI does OE represent?

Capitalization

The capitalization rate is determined using the comparable approach and applying it to income-producing properties. To determine comparables, find properties similar to the subject property, determine their NOI and their sales price, and divide.

CAP rate = NOI ÷ sales price

▶ *Tip*

If there is more than one comparable, average the NOIs and sales prices, and then divide.

CAP Rate Example:
If the comparable sold for $756,000 and its NOI was $82,720, its CAP rate would be:

$82,720 (NOI) ÷ $756,000 (sales price) = .109 (CAP rate)

PUT YOUR CAPITALIZATION RATE CALCULATION SKILLS TO WORK

5. Calculate the CAP rate if the comparable sold for $123,000 and its NOI is $27,302.

Market Value

The hard work is done. As we said at the start:

NOI ÷ CAP rate = estimated market value

Market Value Example:

We won't redo the preliminaries here, but will just assume an NOI of $16,300 and a CAP rate of .107.

$16,300 ÷ 10.7% = $152,336.45

PUT YOUR MARKET VALUE CALCULATION SKILLS TO WORK

6. Determine the estimated value of a property with an NOI of $27,000 and a CAP rate of 11.3%.

7. Assume two comparables, the first with a selling price of $232,900 and NOI of $29,125, and the second with a selling price of $263,700 and NOI of $31,725. All things being equal, what is the estimated market value of the subject property around the corner if it has an NOI of $33,622?

CALCULATING MARKET VALUE USING GROSS RENT AND INCOME MULTIPLIER APPROACH

The gross rent multiplier (GRM) is determined by dividing the selling price of a property by the annual rental income, assuming full rental or anticipated rent. The gross income multiplier (GIM) is essentially the same, except it will include other income, if any, generated from the property—for example, income from a concession in addition to rental income.

The formulas are:

GRM = selling price ÷ monthly or annual full/anticipated rent

GIM = selling price ÷ (monthly or annual full/anticipated rent + full/anticipated other income)

Similarly, the formulas for estimated market value are:

estimated market value = monthly or annual full/anticipated rent × GRM

estimated market value = (monthly or annual full/anticipated rent + annual/anticipated other income) × GIM

This method is far rougher than the direct capitalization method, but can provide a quick analysis. It becomes somewhat more accurate when used in conjunction with comparable sales.

► *Tip*

Neither calculation accounts for operating expenses, depreciation, and condition of the property.

Gross Rent/Income Multiplier Example:

If the selling price of a small apartment building with annual gross rents of $48,000 per year is $425,000, the GRM is:

$425,000 ÷ $48,000 = 8.85

Taking the same building and adding annual gross additional income of $7,500, the GIM would be:

$425,000 ÷ ($48,000 + $7,500) =

$425,000 ÷ $55,500 = 7.658

To get the estimated market value of a property, where an average of comparable GRMs is 8.25 and the anticipated rent of $72,000 is based on comparables, perform the following calculation:

$72,000 × 8.25 = $594,000

PUT YOUR GROSS RENT/INCOME MULTIPLIER CALCULATION SKILLS TO WORK

8. On a property selling for $475,000, the gross income is $5,000 per month and additional income is $575 per month. Calculate the monthly GRM and the annual GIM.

9. If the comparables are:

Selling Price	Annual Rental	Annual GRM
$625,796	$69,445	
$639,900	$79,000	
$652,800	$83,000	
Average GRM		

Figure 8.1

determine the GRM for each and then calculate the average GRM.

10. Based on the GRM in the previous exercise, what should be the estimated selling price of a subject property with an annual rent roll of $82,575?

CALCULATING MARKET VALUE USING DISCOUNTED CASH FLOW APPROACH

Multiple years of NOI can be valued using a discounted cash flow analysis (DCF) model. Probably the most difficult thing to understand about DCF is the idea of **discounted value** or **present value**. Essentially, it means what tomorrow's money is worth in today's dollars. If you invest in a property today, how much would you have to earn for that investment to be worthwhile?

Discounted Cash Flow Example:

Let's assume you received an income of $10,000 per year on your investment. At the end of five years, assuming a discount rate of 5%, you would have earned $43,294.87 in today's dollars.

End of Year	Cash Flow	÷ by Discount (1.05 × 1.05 for each year)	Discounted Value
1	$10,000	1.0500	$9,523.81
2	$10,000	1.1025	$9,070.29
3	$10,000	1.1576	$8,638.56
4	$10,000	1.2155	$8,227.07
5	$10,000	1.2763	$7,835.15
Total			$43,294.88

Figure 8.2

To keep the numbers simple, let's assume you invested in a property today, and at the end of five years, you not only received $10,000 per year, but also realized a gain of $100,000.

End of Year	Cash Flow	÷ by Discount (1.05 × 1.05 for each year)	Discounted Value
1	$10,000	1.0500	$9,523.81
2	$10,000	1.1025	$9,070.29
3	$10,000	1.1576	$8,638.56
4	$10,000	1.2155	$8,227.07
5	$110,000	1.2763	$86,186.63
Total			$121,646.36

Figure 8.3

If the initial investment in the property was $75,000 and had been put into T-bills at 5% (a very safe investment), compounded, the money would have been worth $95,721.12 after five years.

End of Year	Cash	Compound Interest	Value
1	$ 75,000	5%	$78,750.00
2	$ 10,000	5%	$82,687.50
3	$ 10,000	5%	$86,821.88
4	$ 10,000	5%	$91,162.97
5	$110,000	5%	$95,721.12

Figure 8.4

Assuming there were no other costs associated with the property, the profit in today's dollars could be calculated as:

$$\frac{\text{current value} - \text{cost}}{\text{cost}} = \text{rate of return}$$

$$\frac{\$121,646.35 - \$95,721.12}{\$95,721.12} = \frac{\$25,925.23}{\$95,721.12} = .271 \text{ or } 27\%$$

▶ *Tip*

None of the valuation methods covered takes into account the condition of the property and future expenses or the condition of comparables. For a general discussion of depreciation and economic life of a property, see Chapter 7. For a discussion of the tax consequences, see Chapter 10.

Now, let's turn it around and assume an investor is calculating what to pay for a property. The required rate of return is 9.5%, the CAP rate is projected to be 9.7%, and the NOI for each year is projected as:

Year	NOI + Reversion (Sale) at End of Fifth Year	× Discount	Present Value at 9.5%
1	$133,000	$\frac{1}{1.095} = .913242$	$121,461.19
2	$135,625	$\frac{1}{(1.095)}2 = .834028$	$113,115.05
3	$138,750	$\frac{1}{(1.095)}3 = .761672$	$105,681.99
4	$142,500	$\frac{1}{(1.095)}4 = .695574$	$99,119.30
5	$145,600	$\frac{1}{(1.095)}5 = .635227$	$92,489.05
Reversion value (year 5)	$1,501,030	$\frac{1}{(1.095)}5 = .635227$	$953,494.78
Total			$1,485,361.36

In the fifth year, NOI is $145,600 and outgoing CAP rate is 9.7%. Use the formula:

NOI ÷ CAP rate = reversion value

$145,600 ÷ .097 = $1,501,030.93 = $1,501,031 (rounded)

Based on these calculations, the present value of the property to the investor would be $2,363,082.50.

► **Tip**

Two methods for calculating discount were used; some differences will result from rounding.

PUT YOUR DISCOUNTED CASH FLOW CALCULATION SKILLS TO WORK

11. Assume an investor sold a property after three years for $125,000. If the discount rate is 7.5%, how much would the investor have had to pay to break even on the investment in present dollars?

End of Year	Cash Flow	÷ by Discount (1.075 × 1.075 for each year)	Discounted Value
1	$125,000	1.075	$116,279.06
2	$125,000	1.156	$108,131.48
3	$125,000	1.242	$100,644.12

12. Let's say the investor had invested the amount derived in question 11, and then sold the property for $175,000. Assuming no additional income or costs, how much did the investor net in present dollars?

ANSWERS

Answers appear in **boldface**.

1. $83,046 (PGI) × 15% (VCL) = $12,456.90 (VCL in $)
   $83,046 − $12,456.90 = **$70,589.10** EGI

2. $70,589.10 (EGI) − $22,330 (OE) = **$48,259.10** NOI

3. $1,650,000 (EGI) − $1,236,792 (NOI) = **$413,208** OE

4. $413,208 ÷ $1,650,000 = **25%** GOI

5. $27,302 (NOI) ÷ $123,000 (selling price) = **.222** CAP rate or (22.2%)

6. $27,000 ÷ .113 = **$238,938.05** estimated property value

7. ($232,900 + $263,700) ÷ 2 = $248,300 (average selling price)
   ($29,125 + 31,725) ÷ 2 = $30,425 (average NOI)
   $30,425 ÷ $248,300 = .1225 (CAP rate)
   $33,622 ÷ .1225 = **$274,465.31** estimated market value

8. $475,000 (selling price) ÷ $5,000 (monthly rent + other income) = monthly GRM
   $475,000 ÷ $5,000 = **95** monthly GRM
   $475,000 ÷ ($5,575 × 12) (annual rent + annual other income) = annual GIM
   $475,000 ÷ $66,900 = **7.1** annual GIM

9.

Selling Price	Annual Rate	Annual GRM
$652,800	$69,495	9.00
$639,900	$79,000	8.10
$652,800	$83,000	7.86
Average GRM		**8.32**

9.00 + 8.10 + 7.86 = 24.96 ÷ 3 = **8.32**

10. $82,575 × 8.32 = **$687,024** estimated selling price

Year	Cash Flow	Discount	Discounted Value
1	$125,000	1.075	$116,279.06
2	$125,000	1.156	$108,038.02
3	$125,000	1.213	$103,050.28

11. **$103,050.28**

12. $175,000 (selling price) ÷ 1.213 (discount after three years) = $144,270.40 (present value)

$144,270.40 – $103,050 = **$41,220.40** profit

PART

IV

INVESTING IN REAL ESTATE

9

EVALUATING INVESTMENT PROPERTY: INCOME

CALCULATING RENTS

There are several types of leases, and the calculations vary a bit.

- **percentage lease** or **retail lease:** Property owner receives a percentage of gross sales in excess of some negotiated amount plus a monthly minimum rent.
- **index lease:** Rent escalates at specified times—for example, every year or every two years at a stipulated rate, or it may be tied to an index like the consumer price index. This type of lease is often used in residential real estate.

Rents may be either:
- **gross rent:** Landlord pays operating expenses, for example, heat and electric.
- **net rent:** Tenant pays expenses; the landlord nets a predictable amount each month.

▶ *Tip*

Annual office and warehouse rent is typically quoted in price per square foot.

Rent Example:

A retail lease calls for a monthly rent of $525 per month plus 2.5% of gross sales over $240,000 per year. Gross sales were $325,000. To calculate the total rent that year:

$525 (monthly rent) × 12 months + .025($325,000 – $240,000) = annual rent

$6,300 + .025($85,000) =

$6,300 + $2,125 = $8,425 annual rent

To calculate the increase on a variable lease where the current monthly rent is $1,750 and the rent is tied to an index that went from 1.3 to 1.55, first determine the rate of increase.

1.55 – 1.3 = .25

.25 ÷ 1.3 = .1923 or 19.23%

To get the new rent, multiply:

$1,750 × .1923 = $336.53

$1,750 + $336.53 = $2,086.53

An easier way to derive this number is to multiply the original rent by 119.23% (or 1.1923):

$1,750 × 1.1923 = $2,086.53

PUT YOUR RENT CALCULATION SKILLS TO WORK

1. An office rents for $15.75 per square foot; increases are tied to an index that has increased from 1.75 to 1.95. The office space is 25,000 square feet. What is the monthly rent?

2. Rents on apartments increase 7% each year. Assuming all rents increase as of January 1, what is the total rental income after two years if the current rents are three apartments at $975 per month, eight apartments at $1,145 per month, and 12 apartments at $1,250 per month?

CALCULATING PRETAX CASH FLOW

In appraising and valuing investment property in Chapter 8, you learned about potential gross income (PGI), operating expenses (OE), and net operating income (NOI). Effective gross income (EGI) is the income produced after vacancy and collection losses (VCL) are subtracted and any other income is added. The formula is:

PGI – VCL + other income = EGI

EGI – OE = NOI

Pretax cash flow (PTCF) is the result of subtracting mortgage payments (principal + interest) from NOI, or:

NOI – mortgage payments = PTCF

Pretax Cash Flow Example:

Assume an investment of $505,505 representing 80% of the purchase price in a residential building with 22 apartments. The mortgage is for 30 years at 6.95%; monthly payments are $3,342.84. The building has 22 apartments: eight studios that each rent for $575 per month, 8 one-bedroom apartments that each rent for $725 per month, 4 two-bedroom apartments that each rent for $900 per month, and 2 three-bedroom apartments that each rent for $1,225 per month. Collection losses are 7.5%, and operating expenses are estimated at 42.5% of EGI.

STEP 1: Compute PGI.

($575 × 8) + ($725 × 8) + ($900 × 4) + ($1,225 × 2) =

$4,600 + $5,800 + $3,600 + $2,450 = $16,450

$16,450 × 12 = $197,400

STEP 2: Calculate VCL.

$197,400 × .075 = $14,805

STEP 3: EGI

$197,400 – $14,805 = $182,595

STEP 4: OE

$182,595 × .425 = $77,602.88

STEP 5: NOI

$182,595 – $77,602.88 = $104,992.13

STEP 6: Annual mortgage payment

$3,342.84 × 12 = $40,114.08

STEP 7: PTCF

$104,992.13 – $40,114.08 = $64,878.05

PUT YOUR PRETAX CASH FLOW CALCULATION SKILLS TO WORK

Assume an investment of $522,600 in a residential building with ten apartments. There is an 80% ($435,000), 30-year mortgage at 7.2% and monthly payments of $2,952.73. The 12 apartments include four studios that each rent for $425 per month, four 1-bedroom apartments that each rent for $600 per month, and four 2-bedroom apartments that each rent for $775 per month. Collection losses are 9%, and operating expenses are estimated at 40% of EGI.

3. What is the PGI?

4. What is the VCL?

5. What is the EGI?

6. What is the OE?

7. What is the NOI?

8. What is the annual mortgage payment?

9. What is the PTCF?

CALCULATING RATES OF RETURN

There are many measures investors use to evaluate an investment. Among the most common are return on investment (ROI), return on equity (ROE) (also called the equity dividend rate), debt service coverage ratio (DSCR), and operating expense ratio (OER).

Note: Throughout this section, we'll be referring to the PTCF example to calculate rates of return.

Return on Investment

This is a calculation of how much the investor earns on the total investment.

NOI ÷ purchase price = ROI

The higher the number, the better the investment is.

ROI Example:

The purchase price was:

$119,671.87 ÷ $505,505 = .23674 = 23.7%

Return on Equity/Cash-on-Cash Return

Equity is the amount of actual money the investor has in the property. The formula is:

PTCF ÷ equity = ROE

The higher the number, the better the investment is.

ROE Example:

We'll assume here that the investor is evaluating the property in the earlier example; therefore, the equity is the down payment and the PTCF is for the projected first year.

The property is selling for $505,505, and the mortgage will be 80%; therefore, the investor's equity is:

$505,505 × .20 = $101,101

PCTF was $79,557.79; therefore, to determine ROE:

$79,557.79 ÷ $101,101 = .78691 = 79%

Debt Service Coverage Ratio

The debt service coverage ratio is the correlation of the NOI to the sum of its annual mortgage payments (annual debt service):

NOI ÷ annual mortgage payment = DSCR

The higher the number, the better the investment is.

Debt Service Coverage Ratio Example:

The annual mortgage payment was $40,114.08, and the NOI was $119,671.87.

$119,671.87 ÷ $40,114.08 = 2.9833 = 298%

Operating Expense

This, of course, measures cost against the property. The formula here is:

OE ÷ EGI = operating expense ratio

Unlike the other ratios, the lower the number, the better the investment is.

Operating Expense Example:

The OE in our example is $88,453.13, and the EGI is $208,125.

$88,453.13 ÷ $208,125 = .425 = 42.5%

All of the ratios were extremely good. Before investing in this property, the investor should probably do some digging to determine whether there is some underlying problem that will require a large investment, or whether there is some other reason for the price being so low in light of the income and level expenses shown. Of course, just maybe, the investor really did find a bargain!

PUT YOUR RATES OF RETURN CALCULATION SKILLS TO WORK

Using the answers to questions 2 through 9 (reminder: selling price was $435,000 with an 80% mortgage, and monthly payments of $2,952.73), calculate the following:

10. ROI

11. ROE

12. DSCR

13. OER

ANSWERS

Answers are in **boldface**.

1. $1.95 - 1.75 = .2$

$.2 \div 1.75 = .1143$ (rounded) or 11.43%

$\$15.75 \times 1.1143 = \$17.55$

$\$17.55 \times 25,000$ sq. ft. $= \$438,750 \div 12 = \textbf{\$36,562.50}$ monthly rent

2. $(3 \times \$975) + (8 \times \$1,145) + (12 \times \$1,250) =$

$\$2,925 + \$9,160 + \$15,000 = \$27,085$ (annual rent all apartments)

$\$27,085 \times 1.07 = \$28,980.95$ first year

$\$28,981 \times 1.07 = \textbf{\$31,009.67}$ second year

3. $[(\$425 \times 4) + (\$600 \times 4) + (\$775 \times 4)] \times 12 =$

$(\$1,700 + \$2,400 + \$3,100) \times 12 =$

$\$7,200 \times 12 = \textbf{\$86,400}$ PGI

4. $\$86,400 \times .09 = \textbf{\$7,776}$ VCL

5. $\$86,400 - \$7,776 = \textbf{\$78,624}$ EGI

6. $\$78,624 \times .40 = \textbf{\$31,449.60}$ (rounded) OE

7. $\$78,624 - \$31,449.60 = \textbf{\$47,174.40}$ NOI

8. $\$2,952.73 \times 12 = \textbf{\$35,432.76}$ annual mortgage payment

9. $\$47,174.40 - \$35,432.76 = \textbf{\$11,741.64}$ PTCF

10. $\$47,174.40$ (NOI) $\div \$435,000 = .10845 = \textbf{10.8\%}$ ROI

11. $\$435,000 \times .20 = \$87,000$ (down payment/equity)

$\$11,741.40$ (PTCF) $\div \$87,000 = .1350 = \textbf{13.5\%}$ ROE

12. $\$47,174.40$ (NOI) $\div \$35,432.76 = 1.3314 = \textbf{133\%}$ DSCR

13. $\$31,449.60 \div \$78,624 = .4 = \textbf{40\%}$ OER

CHAPTER

10

EVALUATING INVESTMENT PROPERTY: APPRECIATION AND DEPRECIATION

CALCULATING DEPRECIATION

Depreciation is the accounting and tax method for considering the cost of wear-and-tear on an asset. Only investment properties qualify for depreciation deductions. Although the property may be increasing in value, IRS requires owners to systematically depreciate the property over its projected useful life span. Real estate depreciation also applies to capital improvements to the building, landscaping, pavements, and so on; however, land may not be depreciated. Neither may everyday repairs and operating costs.

The amount of depreciation depends on the investor's capital investment, with some portion, if necessary, deducted for the value of the land, which is not depreciable. In addition, all other capital investments may also be depreciated. Depreciable improvements are any work that contributes to the property's value or extends the property's useful life.

According to IRS rules, real estate depreciation starts when the property goes into service—that is, it must be available for occupancy or tenancy; it does not have to be occupied for depreciation to begin. In addition, depreciation does not necessarily begin when the property is purchased; for example, an individual investor may own a home, decide to move to another state, and instead of selling the home, decide to rent it. The property would then be depreciable.

Investment real estate that the taxpayer has purchased and *placed into service* after January 1, 1987, uses the Modified Accelerated Cost Recovery System (MACRS) to calculate depreciation. This system is used in this book to illustrate depreciation.

Residential real estate includes apartment buildings, condominium units, cooperative units, and houses rented as residences for tenants, but not hotels, resorts, etc. Residential real estate is depreciated over 27.5 years using the straight-line method (see Chapter 7). All other real estate is depreciated using the straight-line method over 39 years, and the formula is:

depreciable basis (capital investment − land) ÷ 27.5 or 39 years = annual depreciation allowance

▶ *Tip*

Mixed-use properties—that is, properties in which the owner resides (normally nondepreciable) or that contain business or rental portions (depreciable)—may be depreciated based on the prorated value of the business or rental portions. To qualify for the more beneficial residential category, the mixed-use building must receive at least 80% of its gross rental income from the residential dwelling units.

Depreciation Example:

First, determine the portion of the purchase price that can be allocated to the land; in this example, let's say 15% of the $445,000 purchase price was for purchase of land.

$445,000 × .85 = $378,250 depreciable basis

If the property is residential, the calculation is:

$378,250 ÷ 27.5 = $13,754.55 annual depreciation

If the property is commercial, the calculation is:

$378,250 ÷ 39 = $9,698.72 annual depreciation

▶ *Tip*

In actually determining depreciation for tax purposes, the month the property was put into use affects the amount of taxes an investor will pay, as do other regulations. The IRS provides tables for determining depreciation deductions on investment real estate at its website, www.irs.gov. In all of the examples in this book, a January date of use and ownership of the property for more than one year are assumed.

PUT YOUR DEPRECIATION CALCULATION SKILLS TO WORK

1. What is the depreciation allowance for a commercial property purchased for $975,000 if the land is valued at $102,500?

2. An owner resides in 20% of an apartment building purchased for $619,900; the land is valued at $82,500. What is the owner's depreciable basis?

Depreciation and Taxable Income

The annual depreciation is deductible from the net income on the property and, therefore, works to reduce other taxes—for example, federal, state, and local taxes.

▶ *Tip*

In addition to depreciation, an investor will usually claim the interest portion of the monthly mortgage payment as a tax deduction.

Depreciation and Taxable Income Example:
Assume:

net operating income	$65,000.00
interest	($28,368.75)
depreciation	($9,698.72)
taxable income	$26,932.53

PUT YOUR DEPRECIATION AND TAX CALCULATION SKILLS TO WORK

3. If a residential building is purchased for $833,333 exclusive of land, annual interest payments are $40,800, and net operating income is $109,025, how much is the taxable income?

CALCULATING AFTER-TAX INCOME FROM SALE

In the previous examples, the amount of money received on reversion or sale of the property after some projected period is included in our calculations. Not included are any allowance for taxes, selling expenses, and so on that may be due.

Two types of taxes are owed if an investor makes money on the sale of property; the first is a tax on the capital gain, and the second is a tax on any gain that may have resulted from excess depreciation—gain is greater than the accumulated tax depreciation previously deducted from tax payments. The current capital gains tax rate is 15%, and on recapture of depreciation it is 25%.

To calculate capital gains, the formula is:

original purchase price – depreciation taken = adjusted basis

sale price – adjusted basis – selling expenses (commissions, transfer taxes, etc.) = capital gain

This is taxed by IRS and may be subject to state and local taxes as well.

To determine excess gain, the formula is:

capital gain – (selling price – purchase price) = excess gain

 ▶ *Tip*

Internal Revenue Code § 1031: "No gain or loss shall be recognized on the exchange of property held for productive use in a trade or business or for investment if such property is exchanged solely for property of like-kind which is to be held either for productive use in a trade or business or for investment."

How well did the investor do after taxes? For that, deduct the remaining mortgage balance, selling expenses, and the taxes owed from the selling price. (In this chapter, because state and local taxes vary, only federal taxes are used to illustrate the examples and exercises.) The formula is:

selling price – mortgage balance – selling expenses – taxes owed = after-tax income

After-Tax Income from Sale Example:

An investor purchases an office building for $838,000. The land is valued at $167,000. After seven years, the property sold for $1,675,000. The selling expenses were $83,750, and the mortgage balance is $601,784.52

STEP 1: Calculate depreciation for seven years on a commercial building.

$838,000 − $167,000 ÷ 39 =

$671,000 ÷ 39 × 7 =

$17,205.13 × 7 = $120,435.91 depreciation taken

STEP 2: Calculate adjusted basis.

$838,000 − $120,435.91 = $717,564.09 adjusted basis

STEP 3: Calculate capital gain.

$1,675,000 − $717,564.09 − $83,750 = $873,686 capital gain

$873,686 × .15 = $131,052.90 capital gains taxes owed

STEP 4: Calculate excess gain.

$873,686 − ($1,675,000 − $838,000) =

$873,000 − $837,000 = $36,000 excess gain

$36,000 × .25 = $9,000

STEP 5: Calculate after-tax cash income.

$1,675,000 − $601,784.52 − $83,750 − $140,052.90 = $849,412.58 after-tax income

PUT YOUR AFTER-TAX INCOME FROM SALE CALCULATION SKILLS TO WORK

A residential building was purchased for $612,000 five years ago. The land was evaluated at $122,400 at time of purchase. The property just sold for $744,591.56. Selling expenses are $44,675.49, and the balance owed on the mortgage is $467,275.49.

4. Calculate depreciation.

5. Calculate adjusted basis.

6. Calculate capital gains tax.

7. Calculate excess gain tax.

8. Calculate after-tax income.

ANSWERS

Answers are in **boldface**.

1. $975,000 (purchase price) – $102,500 (cost of land) = $872,500 (depreciable basis)

    $872,500 ÷ 39 = **$22,371.79** annual depreciation

2. $619,900 (purchase price) – $82,500 = $537,400

    $537,400 × 80% = $429,920 (depreciable basis)

    $429,920 ÷ 27.5 = **$15,633.45** depreciable basis

3. $833,333 (depreciable basis; price did not include land) ÷ 27.5 = $30,303.02 (depreciation)

    $109,025 (net operating income) – $40,800 (interest) – $30,303.02 = **$37,921.98** taxable income

4. [$612,000 (purchase price) – $122,400 (value of land)] ÷ 27.5 =

    $489,600 ÷ 27.5 × 5 = **$89,018.18** depreciation taken

5. $612,000 (original purchase price) – $124,625.48 (depreciation taken) = **$487,374.52** adjusted basis

6. $744,591.56 (selling price) – $487,374.52 (adjusted basis) – $44,675.49 (selling expense) = $212,541.55 (capital gain)

    $212,541.55 × .15 = **$31,881.23** capital gains tax

7. $212,541.55 (capital gain) – [$744,591.56 (selling price) – $612,000 (purchase price)]

    $212,541.55 – $132,591,56 = $79,949.99 excess gain

    $79,949.99 × .25 = **$19,987.50** excess gain tax

8. $744,591.56 (selling price) – $467,275.49 (mortgage balance) – $44,675.49 (selling expenses) – $31,881.23 – $19,987.48 (taxes owed) = **$180,771.87** after-tax income

CLOSING
THE SALE

CALCULATING CLOSING COSTS

The closing statement is, in effect, a balance sheet for the sale of the property. It summarizes all the amounts credited and debited to the buyer and seller. The list of items on a closing statement seems to go on forever. Here is a summary of the most common:

- *attorney (lawyer) fees,* paid by either or both parties
- *transfer taxes* paid by either or both parties
- *survey fee* paid by either party
- *broker's commissions,* usually paid by the seller, may be paid by the buyer. Commissions may be split between two brokers if the "listing agent" and the "selling agent" are from different real estate companies.
- *mortgage application fees,* paid by the buyer to the lender to cover the costs of processing their loan application. These fees may have been paid prior to the closing.
- *points,* paid by either the buyer or the seller to the lender

- *appraisal fees*, paid by the buyer or the seller, depending on the market
- *inspection fees*, usually paid by the buyer
- *home warranties*, negotiable
- *title and escrow fees*, paid by either party, or both, according to the contract
- *prepaid property insurance*, paid by the buyer

Settlement statements may vary, but in general they look something like and contain information similar to Figure 11.1. We've discussed in earlier chapters how to calculate most of these charges. In this chapter, we'll examine how to calculate pro rata charges, commissions, and title charges.

NAME AND ADDRESS OF BORROWER:	NAME AND ADDRESS OF SELLER:		NAME AND ADDRESS OF LENDER:	
PROPERTY LOCATION:	SETTLEMENT AGENT: NAME AND ADDRESS			
	PLACE OF SETTLEMENT:		SETTLEMENT DATE:	

SUMMARY OF BORROWER'S TRANSACTION		SUMMARY OF SELLER'S TRANSACTION	
GROSS AMOUNT DUE FROM BORROWER:		**GROSS AMOUNT DUE TO SELLER:**	
Contract sales price		Contract sales price	
Personal property		Personal property	
Settlement charges to borrower (line 1400)			
Adjustments for items paid by seller in advance		*Adjustments for items paid by seller in advance*	
City/town taxes to		City/town taxes to	
County taxes to		County taxes to	
Assessments to		Assessments to	
GROSS AMOUNT DUE FROM BORROWER		**GROSS AMOUNT DUE TO SELLER**	
AMOUNTS PAID BY OR IN BEHALF OF BORROWER:		**REDUCTIONS IN AMOUNT DUE TO SELLER:**	
Deposit of earnest money		Excess deposit	
202. Principal amount of new loan(s)		Settlement charges to seller (line 1400)	
203. Existing loan(s) taken subject to		Existing loan(s) taken subject to	
		Payoff of first mortgage loan	
		Payoff of second mortgage loan	
Adjustments for items unpaid by seller		*Adjustments for items unpaid by seller*	
City/town taxes to		City/town taxes to	
County taxes to		County taxes to	
Assessments to		Assessments to	
TOTAL PAID BY/FOR BORROWER		**TOTAL REDUCTION AMOUNT DUE TO SELLER**	
CASH AT SETTLEMENT FROM/TO BORROWER		**CASH AT SETTLEMENT TO/FROM SELLER**	
Gross amount due from borrower		Gross amount due to seller	
Less amounts paid by/for borrower		Less reductions in amount due to seller	
CASH (__ FROM) (__TO) BORROWER		**CASH (__TO) (__FROM) SELLER**	

Figure 11.1

Figure 11.1 Settlement Worksheet
Adapted from U.S. Department of Housing and Urban Development Settlement Statement
Source: http://www.hud.gov/offices/hsg/sfh/res/sc3sectd.cfm

SETTLEMENT CHARGES		
TOTAL SALES/BROKER'S COMMISSION **based on price $ @ %=**	PAID FROM BORROWER'S FUNDS AT SETTLEMENT	PAID FROM SELLER'S FUNDS AT SETTLEMENT
Division of Commission as follows:		
$ to		
$ to		
Commission paid at settlement		
ITEMS PAYABLE IN CONNECTION WITH LOAN		
Loan origination fee %		
Loan discount %		
Appraisal fee to		
Credit report to		
Lender's inspection fee		
Mortgage insurance application fee to		
Assumption fee		
ITEMS REQUIRED BY LENDER TO BE PAID IN ADVANCE		
Interest from to @ $/day		
Mortgage insurance premium for months to		
Hazard insurance premium for years to		
RESERVES DEPOSITED WITH LENDER		
Hazard insurance months @ $ per month		
Mortgage insurance months @ $ per month		
City property taxes months @ $ per month		
County property taxes months @ $ per month		
Annual assessments months @ $ per month		
months @ $ per month		
months @ $ per month		
Aggregate adjustment months @ $ per month		
TITLE CHARGES		
Settlement or closing fee to		
Abstract or title search to		
Title examination to		
Title insurance binder to		
Document preparation to		
Notary fees to		
Attorney's fees to		
(includes above items numbers)		
Title insurance to		
(includes above items numbers)		
Lender's coverage $		
Owner's coverage $		

Figure 11.1 (continued)

GOVERNMENT RECORDING AND TRANSFER CHARGES		
Recording fees: Deed $; Mortgage $; Releases $		
City/county tax/stamps: Deed $; Mortgage $		
State tax/stamps: Deed $; Mortgage $		
1300. **ADDITIONAL SETTLEMENT CHARGES**		
1301. Survey to		
1302. Pest inspection to		
1400. **TOTAL SETTLEMENT CHARGES** (*enter on lines 103, Section J and 502, Section K*)		

Figure 11.1 (continued)

CALCULATING PRO RATA CHARGES AND CREDITS

At closing, there are a number of costs that are generally shared between buyer and seller on a pro rata basis; among them are:

- *Property taxes:* Most (but not all) jurisdictions assess taxes on real property, which are usually payable at specified dates annually, biannually, or quarterly.
- *Homeowners association dues,* if applicable. Dues assessed against each property owner are prorated at closing.
- *Interest* on the monthly mortgage payment is calculated and payable on a specified day each month.
- *Rental income* received by the seller is prorated as of the close of the escrow date for the remaining portion of the rental period, usually a month.

 ▶ *Tip*

As a rule, property taxes are paid in arrears; that is, they are paid at the end of the tax period rather than at the beginning. Therefore, the seller must reimburse the buyer for the period the seller owned the property.

▶ *Tip*

Mortgage payments are generally made monthly and, as a rule, are paid at the first of the month. If the seller's mortgage is being assumed by the buyer, the seller must reimburse the buyer for the time the seller had use of the property. More often than not, the mortgage is not being assumed, and therefore, the buyer will have to pay the lender any interest owed to the closing date. This is in addition to repaying the unpaid balance due on the mortgage.

Security deposits are transferred in full to the new owner.

Oil, gas, and water bills:

No matter what the charge is for, before you begin the calculation, ask:

- How many months has the seller paid for?
- How many months has the seller used?
- How many months should the seller be reimbursed for?
- How many months will the buyer use?
- How many months has the buyer paid for?
- How many months should the buyer reimburse the seller for?

▶ *Tip*

Rent is usually paid in advance; as of the date of closing, the remaining portion of the rental income belongs to the buyer.

365-Day Approach

Identify the number of calendar days covered by the bill, and divide the cost by the number of days to get the daily amount. Then, multiply the daily amount by the number of days up to and including the day of closing.

▶ *Tip*

Add a day in February if it is a leap year.

This is done using the formula:

total $ amount ÷ 365 = daily $ amount

daily $ amount × number of days = prorated $ amount

which can be combined as follows:

(number of days ÷ 365) × yearly $ amount =

365-Day Example:

For example, assume the estimated property taxes on a home are $3,200, and that the taxes are paid annually on January 1 for the preceding year. The closing is on August 18, and the seller will be responsible for the taxes through August 17. To determine how much the seller will have to reimburse the buyer:

$3,200 ÷ 365 =

$8.7671233 × 229 days (January 1–August 17) = $2,007.67 (rounded)

Using the combined method, the equation would look like

(229 ÷ 365) × $3,200 = .06273972 × $3,200 = $2,007.67 (rounded)

Tip

Taxes are generally paid in arrears, and custom varies as to how money is prorated when the bill is only an estimate.

PUT YOUR 365-DAY CALCULATION SKILLS TO WORK

Assuming the closing is on June 17, property taxes paid in arrears annually are $8,237. The closing date is the buyer's responsibility.

1. For how many days does the seller owe the buyer?

2. What is the average cost per day?

3. How much does the seller owe the buyer?

4. Using the previous 365-day example (taxes = $3,200, closing date May 17, seller responsible through May 16), assume that payment is made in two equal installments on March 15 for the period November 1 (of the preceding year)–April 30 and September 15 for the period May 1–October 31. How much is the seller's share?

5. Assume there is a building with a rent roll of $27,650 per month, collected on the 1st. Closing is on July 12. The seller retains the income for day of closing. How much does the seller have to reimburse the buyer?

6. Water bills are averaging $250 per quarter and are paid in advance: January 1, April 1, July 1, and October 1. The closing is November 23rd. How much will the buyer need to reimburse the seller? The seller will pay for the day of closing.

30-Day Month Method

This method is less accurate, but simpler to use. The assumption is that each month has 30 days, including February. Using this method, the formula becomes:

total $ amount ÷ 30 = daily $ amount

daily $ amount × number of days = prorated $ amount

When determining an annual rate, substitute 360 (number of days in year) to get the daily rate.

> *30-Day Example:*
> Assume a building with a rent roll of $2,765 per month collected on the 1st. Closing is on July 12. The seller retains the income for the day of closing. How much does the seller have to reimburse the buyer?
> ($2,765 ÷ 30) × 18 =
> $92.166666 × 18 = $1,659

PUT YOUR 30-DAY CALCULATION SKILLS TO WORK

Assuming the closing is on June 17, property taxes paid in arrears annually are $8,237. The closing date is the buyer's responsibility.

7. For how many days does the seller owe the buyer?

8. What is the average cost per day?

9. How much does the seller owe the buyer?

10. Yearly taxes are $17,225 on a small office building. They are paid in arrears quarterly on the last day of the month. The closing date is February 28. This is a leap year. Using the 30-day method, how much does the seller owe the buyer if the seller is responsible for the closing date?

Calculating Commissions

Of these, the only one that requires calculation is the broker's commission. Broker's commissions vary from market to market and deal to deal. Sometimes commissions must be divided—usually 50–50 between listing and selling offices, which often are different firms; then they are further divided to pay the sales associate(s). These formulas are straightforward.

> selling price × commission rate = total commission paid
>
> total commission ÷ sales associate's commission rate = sales associate's commission

▶ *Tip*

If two or more firms split the commission, after calculating the total commission, determine the brokerage firm's commission rate.

Total commission paid divided by brokerage firm's commission rate equals brokerage firm's commission, and then calculate the sales associate's commission based on each firm's receipts.

Things get more complicated when—as is common—the sales associate's commission is based on achieving certain total sales plateaus; such as 50% on the first $400,000, 55% from $400,001–$600,000, and so on. Sometimes, brokers will agree to a graduated commission structure depending on the price at which the property is sold—for example, 5% on the first 500,000, 6% on the next $100,000, and 7% on everything over $601,000.

To calculate, these graduated payments the formula is:

> selling price × 5% (first increment) + 6% of (second increment)
>
> = total of first increment + 7% (balance) = total commission

Commission Example:

The broker's commission is 6% of the selling price, $363,500; the sales associate's commission is at 52.5%.

> $363,500 × .06 = $21,810 total commission
>
> $21,810 × .525 = $11,450.25 sales associate's commission

If the commission had been split with another firm 50–50:

> $21,810 × .5 = $10,905 shared commission
>
> $10,905 × .525 = $5,725.13 (rounded) sales associate's commission

Assume an office building sold for $1,000,000. The commission structure, based on the selling price, is 5% up to $500,000, 6% on the next $250,000, and 7% on the remainder. Because the building sold for $1,000,000, the first step is to determine how much is paid at each rate.

$1,000,000 sales price × $500,000 @ 5% × $250,000 @ 6% = $250,000 remainder @ 7%

Therefore, the formula would look like this:

($500,000 × .05) + ($250,000 × .06) + ($250,000 × .07) = total commission

$25,000 + $15,000 + $17,500 = $57,500

PUT YOUR COMMISSION CALCULATION SKILLS TO WORK

A home is listed at $495,000 and sells for $472,500. Calculate:

11. the total commission at 6%

12. the commission for each brokerage if split 50–50% between two brokerage agencies

13. the listing sales associate's commission at 50%

14. the selling sales associate's commission at 53.5%

15. A seller wants to net $75,000 after commission. The mortgage balance is $200,000. The agent's commission is 6%. Assuming no other costs, how much would the property have to sell for to achieve this goal?

CALCULATING OTHER SETTLEMENT CHARGES

Many fees vary from state to state. In some states, the fees are set by law; in others, they are not. In many states, each title company sets its own rates, which are filed with the state insurance commissioner, and must be followed. In other states, there is a promulgated rate, which is the *minimum* amount the title company is allowed to charge.

According to Quicken Loans (http://www.quickenloans.com/mortgage-news/article/630.html) as of June 2007, the following is a rough estimate of average costs:

- appraisal: up to $450
- credit report: up to $30
- closing fee: up to $400
- title company title search or exam fee: varies greatly
- survey fee: up to $400
- flood determination or life of loan coverage: up to $20
- courier fee: up to $30
- lender's policy title insurance: up to $875
- owner's policy title insurance: up to $875
- homeowners insurance: $300 and up
- buyer's attorney fee (not required in all states): $400 and up
- lender's attorney fee (not required in all states): $150 and up
- escrow deposit for property taxes and mortgage insurance: varies widely
- transfer taxes: varies widely by state and municipality
- recording fees: varies widely depending on municipality
- processing fee: up to $1,000
- underwriting fee: up to $795

ANSWERS

Answers appear in **boldface**.

1. 31 (January) + 28 (February) + 31 (March) + 30 (April) + 31 (May) + 16 (June) = **167** days

2. $8,237 ÷ 365 = **$22.567123** average cost per day

3. $22.567123 × 167 = **$3,768.71** owed to buyer (rounded)

4. $8.7671232 × 75 days (August 17–October 31) = **$657.53** (rounded)

5. ($27,650 ÷ 31) = $891.93 × 19 days = **$16,946.67** reimbursed to buyer

6. ($250 ÷ 92) × 54 = 2.7173913 × 54 = **$146.74** reimbursed to seller (rounded)

7. 5 months at 30 days + 16 days in June = **166** days

8. $8,237 ÷ 360 = **$22.880556** average cost to per day

9. **$3,798.17** owed to buyer (rounded)

10. $17,225 ÷ 360 = $47.847222
30 (January) + 30 (February) = 60 days
$47.847222 × 60 = **$2,870.83** owed to buyer (rounded)

11. $472,500 × .06 = **$28,350** total commission

12. $28,350 × .5 = **$14,175** commission if split 50–50

13. $14,175 × .5 = **$7,087.50** first sales associate's commission

14. $14,175 × .535 = **$7,583.63** (rounded) the second sales associate's commission at 53.5%

15. 100% (total selling price) – 6% (total commission) = 94%
$200,000 (mortgage balance) + $75,000 (to seller) = $275,000
$275,000 ÷ .94 = **$292,553.19**

POSTTEST

This test follows the same format as the pretest you took at the beginning of this book. Again, read each question carefully before you answer it (use scratch paper for your calculations). The answers, including how the problem was calculated, appear at the end of the chapter. If you still have difficulty with a particular type of problem, review the chapter in which that topic is covered.

1. In dollars, what is the maximum PITI someone with an income of $85,000 and long-term debt of $7,500 could qualify for if applying for a conventional mortgage?

2. The buyer is putting 15% down, the PMI is .0075%, and the selling price of the house is $247,500. Calculate the amount of cash the buyer will need.

3. On a $132,000 loan, if the interest rate is 7.8%, what are the annual payments?

4. Let's assume you have a fixed-rate 15-year mortgage and your interest rate is 7.75%. In the first six months of the year, you paid $6,200 interest. How much did you borrow?

5. Find the term of a $450,000 loan where the rate of interest was 8.75% and $42,000 has been paid.

6. If an FHA lender will lend a borrower $230,000 for a rate of 6.8% on a 30-year fixed-rate mortgage, the conventional rate is 7.75%. How many points must the conventional lender charge to meet the FHA rate?

7.

AMORTIZATION SCHEDULE: 30 YEARS TO REPAY $400,000 AT 6.5%				
Payment Number	Payment Amount	Interest Amount	Principal Reduction	Balance Due
84	$971.80	6.5		$ 138,796.17
85				

The monthly payment on the mortgage is $971.80. At the end of seven years, the balance due is $138,796.17. Calculate the balance due after payment 85.

8. Find the monthly payment on a $399,000, 25-year mortgage, where the loan constant is .0070208.

9. Calculate the down payment of a home if the purchase price is $372,500 and the LTV is 77.3.

10. The taxes on a farm in Montgomery Township are 23 mills per $1 of assessed valuation for the town and 9 mills for the school district. Assessed valuation is $99,950. Calculate the total taxes due.

11. The state offers a homeowners exemption of $17,500; the home's assessed value is $243,250. The total tax rate is 12.5 mills. Calculate the total property tax.

12. Assume a monthly mortgage payment of $1,549.39 on a 30-year $226,000 mortgage. Calculate the monthly charge for PMI. Assuming no hazard insurance is required, what is the monthly payment?

13. A 3,400-square-foot condo is listed at $1,450,000. How much per square foot is it selling for?

14. A corner property is shaped like a triangle. The base measures 350 yards, the sides measure 200 yards each. Calculate the square footage and convert it into acres.

15. Replacement costs on a home are estimated as follows: kitchen and bathrooms, 20' × 12' at $125/square foot; remaining living space, 37' × 82' at $85/square foot; an attached garage, 19' × 21' at $37.50/square foot; and finished walkout basement, 27' × 62' at $55/square foot. Calculate the total replacement cost.

16. If a building has an annual depreciation rate of 2.75%, what is its economic life?

17. If the building in question 16 is 22 years old, what is its accrued rate of depreciation?

18. If a dwelling's economic life is 110 years, what is its annual accrued depreciation rate?

19. If the replacement value of the dwelling in question 18 is $633,500, and it is 13 years old, what is its accrued depreciation expressed in dollars?

20. The NOI of an apartment complex is $2,362,000. If the gross operating income is $3,000,000, how much are the operating expenses?

21. What percentage of GOI does that represent?

22. Determine the property value of a property with an NOI of $108,000 and a CAP rate of .119.

23. Assume two comparables, the first with a selling price of $673,050 and NOI of $72,100, and the second with a selling price of $663,700 and NOI of $68,725. All things being equal, what is the estimated market value of the property next door if it has an NOI of $69,900?

24.

Selling Price	Annual Rental	Annual GRM
$697,500	$74,035	
$702,300	$85,750	
$687,600	$71,690	
Average GRM		

Using these comparables, determine the GRM for each and then calculate the average GRM.

25. Based on the GRM in question 24, what should the estimated selling price of a subject property with a rent roll of $78,975 be?

26. Rents on apartments increase 6.5% each year. Assuming all rents increase as of January 1, what is the total rental income after two years if the current rents are three apartments at $800 per month, eight apartments at $1,150 per month, and 12 apartments at $1,325 per month?

Use the following to answer questions 27–30.

Assume an investment of $1,435,000 in a residential building with ten apartments. There is an 80%, 30-year mortgage at 7.2% and monthly payments of $9,740.61. The annual PGI is $442,400; VCL is $55,300; EGI is $387,100; OE is $154,840; NOI is $232,260; yearly mortgage is $116,887.32; BCTF is $115,372.68.

27. Calculate ROI.

28. Calculate ROE.

29. Calculate DSC.

30. Calculate OER.

31. What is the depreciation allowance for a commercial property purchased for $625,000 if the land is valued at $85,500?

32. If a residential building is purchased for $977,779 exclusive of land, annual interest payments are $63,715, and net operating income is $163,025, how much is the taxable income?

Use the following to answer questions 33–37.

A commercial building was purchased for $4,300,000 sixteen years ago. The land was evaluated at $125,000 at time of purchase. The property just sold for $53,000,000. Selling expenses are $4,225,000 and the balance owed on the mortgage is $3,017,634.27.

33. Calculate depreciation.

34. Calculate adjusted basis.

35. Calculate capital gains tax.

36. Calculate excess gain tax.

37. Calculate after-tax income.

Use the following to answer questions 38–40.

A closing is held on September 17, and property taxes paid in arrears annually are $27,420. The closing date is the buyer's responsibility. Using the 365-day method, calculate:

38. How many days does the seller owe the buyer?

39. What is the average cost per day?

40. How much does the seller owe the buyer?

Use the following to answer questions 41–43.

Using the 365-day method, assume annual taxes of $4,325. Payment is made in quarterly installments on March 15 for the period November 1 (of the preceding year)–January 31; June 15 for February 1–April 30; September 15, for May 1–July 31; and September 15 for August 1–October 31. Closing date is July 24, and the seller is responsible through July 23.

41. How many days does the seller owe the buyer?

42. What is the average cost per day?

43. How much does the seller owe the buyer?

44. An apartment building with a rent roll of $62,650 per month, collected on the 1st, is closing on January 18. The seller retains the income for day of closing. How much does the seller have to reimburse the buyer?

45. Water and sewer bills are averaging $327 per quarter and are paid in advance on January 1, April 1, July 1, and October 1. The closing is April 6. How much will the buyer need to reimburse the seller? The buyer will pay for the day of closing.

Use the following to answer questions 46–50.

A home sells for $1,637,500. Calculate the following:

46. the total commission, if the first $500,000 is at 5.5%, the second $500,000 is at 6%, and the balance is 6.5%

47. the commission, if split 50–50 between two brokerage agencies

48. the first sales associate's commission, at 50% on the first $25,000 and 52.5% on the balance

49. the second sales associate's commission at 52.5%

50. the total amount due to seller

ANSWERS

Answers appear in **boldface**.

1. $85,000 (annual income) ÷ 12 = $7,083.33 (monthly income)

$7,500 (annual long-term debt) ÷ 12 = $625 (monthly debt)

$7,083.33 × .28 = $1,983.33

($7,083.33 × .36) − $625 =

$2,550 − $625 = **$1,925** (the lower of the two qualifiers)

2. $247,500 (selling price) × .15 = $37,125 (down payment)

$247,500 − $37,125 = $210,375 (mortgage)

$210,375 × .0075 = $1,578 (PMI)

$1,578 + $37,125 = **$38,703** cash

3. I = P ($132,000) × R (7.8%) × T (1 year)

$132,000 × 7.8% × 1 =

$132,000 × .078 × 1 =

$10,296 annual payments

4. $P = \dfrac{I\,(\$6,200)}{R\,(7.75\%) \times T\,(6\ \text{months})}$

$= \dfrac{6,200}{7.75\% \times .5}$

$= \$6,200 \times (.0775 \times .5)$

$= \$6,200 \times .03875$

$= $ **$160,000** borrowed

5. $T = \dfrac{I\,(\$42,000)}{P\,(\$450,000) \times R\,(8.75\%)}$

$= \dfrac{\$42,000}{\$450,000 \times .0875}$

$= \$42,000 \times (\$450,000 \times .0875)$

$= \$42,000 \times \$39,375 = 1.067$

$= $ **1 year 24 days** (365 × .06)

6. 7.75% − 6.8% = .95%

= .95 discount points = **1 point**

7. $138,796.17 \times .065 \div 12 = \$751.81$ (interest)
$971.80 - \$751.81 = \$219.99$ (toward principal)
$138,796.17 - \$219.99 = \mathbf{\$138,576.18}$ balance due

8. $399,000 \times .0070208 = \$2,801.299 = \mathbf{\$2,801.30}$ monthly payment (rounded)

9. $372,500$ (purchase price) $\times 77.3\%$ (LTV) $=$ (down payment)
$372,500 \times .773 = \mathbf{\$481,888.74}$ down payment

10. 23 mills $= .023$
9 mills $= .009$
$.023 + .009 = .032$
$99,950$ (assessed value) $\times .032 = \mathbf{\$3,198.40}$ taxes due

11. $243,250$ (assessed value) $- \$17,500$ (homestead exemption) $= \$225,750$
(taxable value)
12.5 mills $= .0125$
$225,750 \times .0125 = \mathbf{\$2,821.88}$ property tax (rounded)

12. 226,000 (total mortgage) $\times .005$ (annual PMI) $= \$113.00$ (annual PMI)
$1,130$ (PMI) $\div 12 = \$94.17$ (monthly PMI)
$1,549.39$ (monthly mortgage) $+ \$94.17 = \mathbf{\$1,643.56}$ monthly payment

13. $1,450,000 \div 3,400$ square feet $= \mathbf{\$426.47}$ per square foot

14. (350 yards $\times$ 200 yards) $\div 2 = 35,000$ square yards
35,000 square yards $\times 9 = 315,000$ square feet
315,000 square feet $\div 43,560 = \mathbf{7.23}$ acres

15. $20' \times 12' = 240$ square feet $\times \$125 = \$30,000$
$37' \times 82' = 3,034$ square feet $\times \$85 = \$257,890$
$19' \times 21' = 399$ square feet $\times \$37.50 = \$14,962.50$
$27' \times 62' = 1,674$ square feet $\times \$55 = \$92,070$
$30,000 + \$257,890 + \$14,962.50 + \$92,070 = \mathbf{\$394,922.50}$ replacement cost

16. $100\% \div 2.75\%$ annual depreciation rate $= \mathbf{36.36}$ years of economic life

17. 22 years $\times 2.75\% = \mathbf{60.5\%}$ accrued depreciation

18. 100% ÷ 110 (years of economic life) = 0.9% annual depreciation rate

19. 0.9% annual depreciation rate × 13 years = 11.7% accrued depreciation
$633,000 × 11.7% = **$74,061** accrued depreciation

20. $3,000,000 (EGI) − $2,362,000 (NOI) = **$638,000** OE

21. $638,000 ÷ $3,000,000 = **21.3%** GOI

22. $108,000 ÷ .119 = **$907,563.03** estimated property value

23. ($673,050 + $663,700) ÷ 2 = $668,375 (average selling price)
($72,100 + 68,725) ÷ 2 = $70,412.50 (average NOI)
$70,412.50 ÷ $668,375 = .105 (CAP rate)
$69,900 × .105 = **$665,714.28** estimated market value

24.

Selling Price ÷	Annual Rental =	Annual GRM
$697,500	$74,035	9.42
$702,300	$85,750	8.19
$687,600	$71,690	9.59
Average GRM		**9.06**

(9.42 + 8.19 + 9.59) ÷ 3 = **9.07** annual GRM

25. $78,975 × 9.06 = **$715,513.50** estimated selling price

26. (3 × $800) + (8 × $1,150) + (12 × $1,325) =
$2,400 + $9,200 + $15,900 = $27,500 (annual rent for all apartments)
$27,500 × .065 = $1,787.50 (1st year)
$1,787.50 + $27,500 = $29,287.50
$29,287.50 × .065 = $1,903.69
$1,903.69 + $29,287.50 = **$31,191.19** total rental income after two years

27. $232,260 (NOI) ÷ $1,435,000 = .16185 = **16.2%** ROI

28. $1,435,000 × .20 = $287,000 (down payment/equity)
$115,372.68 (BTCF) ÷ $287,000 = .40200 = **40.2%** ROE

29. $232,260 (NOI) ÷ $116,887.32= 1.9870 = **199%** DSC

30. $154,840 ÷ $387,100 = .4 = **40%** OER

31. $625,000 (purchase price) − $85,500 (cost of land) = $539,500 (depreciable basis)
$539,500 ÷ 39 = **$13,833** annual depreciation

32. $977,779 (depreciable basis; price did not include land) × 27.5 = $35,555.60 (depreciation)
$163,025 (net operating income) − $63,715 (interest) − $35,555.60 = **$63,754.40** taxable income

33. $4,300,000 (purchase price) − $125,000 (value of land) × 39 =
$4,175,000 × 39 × 16 = $107,051.28
$107,051.28 × 16 = **$1,712,820.40** depreciation taken

34. $4,300,000 (original purchase price) − $1,712,820.40 (depreciation taken) = **$2,587,179.60** adjusted basis

35. $53,000,000 (selling price) − $2,587,179.60 (adjusted basis) − $4,225,000 (selling expense) = $46,187,820.40 (capital gain)
$46,187,820.40 × .15 = **$6,928,173.06** capital gains tax

36. $46,187,821 (capital gain) − [$53,000,000 (selling price) − $4,300,000 (purchase price)] =
$46,187,820.40 − $48,700,000 = $4,300,000 (excess gain)
$4,300,000 × .25 = **$1,075,000** excess gains tax

37. $53,000,000 (selling price) − $3,017,634.27 (mortgage balance) − $4,225,000 (selling expenses) − $6,928,173.10 − 1,075,000 (taxes owed) = **$37,754,192.63** after-tax income

38. 31 (January) + 28 (February) + 31 (March) + 30 (April) + 31 (May) + 30 (June) + 31 (July) + 31 (August) + 16 (September) = **259** days

39. $27,420 ÷ 365 = **$75.12** average cost per day

40. $75.830135 × 259 = **$19,640** owed to buyer

41. 31 (May) + 30 (June) + 23 (July) = **84** days

42. $4,325 ÷ 365 = **$11.85** cost per day

43. 11.849315 ÷ 84 = **$995.34** owed to buyer

44. $62,650 ÷ 31 = $2,020.9677
$2,020.9677 × 18 = **$36,377.42** owed to buyer

45. ($327 ÷ 91) × 6 =
3.5934066 × 6 = **$21.56**

46. $500,000 × .055 = $27,500
$500,000 × .06 = $30,000
$637,500 × 0.065 = $41,437.50
$27,500 + $30,000 + $41,437.50 = **$98,937.50** total commission

47. $98,937.50 ÷ 2 = **$49,468.75** 50–50 split commission

48. $49,468.75 − $25,000 = $24,468.75
$25,000 × .5 = $12,500
$24,468.75 × .525 = $12,846.09
$12,500 + $12,846.09 = **$25,346.09** commission

49. $49,468.75 × .525 = **$25,971.09** commission

50. 100% (total selling price) − 6% (total commission) = 94%
$502,750 (mortgage balance) + $1,000,000 (to seller) = $1,502,750
$1,502,750 ÷ .94 = **$1,598,670.21** due to seller

REAL ESTATE GLOSSARY

One of the most basic components in preparing for your real estate exam is making sure you know all the terminology. This glossary provides a list of the most commonly used real estate terms and their definitions.

These terms will help you not only as you study for your real estate exam, but also after you pass your exam and are practicing in the field. The terms are listed in alphabetical order for easy reference.

▶ A

abandonment the voluntary surrender of a right, claim, or interest in a piece of property without naming a successor as owner or tenant.

abstract of title a certified summary of the history of a title to a particular parcel of real estate that includes the original grant and all subsequent transfers, encumbrances, and releases.

abutting sharing a common boundary; adjoining.

accelerated depreciation a way to write off depreciation faster than the traditional straight-line method, in order to lessen tax burden.

acceleration clause a clause in a note, mortgage, or deed of trust that permits the lender to declare the entire amount of principal and accrued interest due and payable immediately in the event of default.

acceptance the indication by a party receiving an offer that they agree to the terms of the offer. In most states, the offer and acceptance must be reduced to writing when real property is involved.

accretion the increase or addition of land resulting from the natural deposit of sand or soil by streams, lakes, or rivers.

accrued depreciation (1) the amount of depreciation, or loss in value, that has accumulated since initial construction; (2) the difference between the current appraised value and the cost to replace the building new.

accrued expense money spent but not yet paid—for example, a repair.

accrued items a list of expenses that have been incurred but have not yet been paid, such as interest on a mortgage loan, that are included on a closing statement.

acknowledgment a formal declaration before a public official, usually a notary public, by a person who has signed a deed, contract, or other document that the execution was a voluntary act.

acquisition cost the price of a piece of property after adjusting for such things as closing costs.

acre a measure of land equal to 43,560 square feet or 4,840 square yards.

actual age chronological age (as opposed to estimated age).

actual eviction the result of legal action brought by a landlord against a defaulted tenant, whereby the tenant is physically removed from rented or leased property by a court order.

actual notice the actual knowledge that a person has of a particular fact.

addendum any provision added to a contract, or an addition to a contract that expands, modifies, or enhances the clarity of the agreement. To be a part of the contract and legally enforceable, an addendum must be referenced within the contract.

adjacent lying near to but not necessarily in actual contact with.

adjoining contiguous or attached; in actual contact with.

adjustable-rate mortgage (ARM) a mortgage in which the interest changes periodically, according to corresponding fluctuations in an index. All ARMs are tied to indexes. For example, a seven-year, adjustable-rate mortgage is a loan in which the rate remains fixed for the first seven years, then fluctuates according to the index to which it is tied.

adjusted basis the original cost of a property, plus acquisition costs, plus the value of added improvements to the property, minus accrued depreciation.

adjusted gross income the amount of money earned from all sources reduced by such things as alimony, contributions to retirement, medical savings accounts, and the like.

adjusted purchase price the sales price plus commissions and other closing costs.

adjusted sales price the sales price less commissions and other closing costs.

adjustment date the date the interest rate changes on an adjustable-rate mortgage.

adjustment interval the amount of time between changes in the interest rate and/or monthly payment on an adjustable rate mortgage.

administrator a person appointed by a court to settle the estate of a person who has died without leaving a will.

ad valorem **tax** tax in proportion to the value of a property.

adverse possession a method of acquiring title to another person's property through court action after taking actual, open, hostile, and continuous possession for a statutory period of time; may require payment of property taxes during the period of possession.

affidavit a written statement made under oath and signed before a licensed public official, usually a notary public.

after-tax cash flow net income plus amortization, depreciation, and other noncash charges.

age-life accrued depreciation method a way to estimate accrued depreciation by dividing a building's effective age by its economic life; an approach used to obtain the replacement cost.

agency the legal relationship between principal and agent that arises out of a contract wherein an agent is employed to do certain acts on behalf of the principal who has retained the agent to deal with a third party.

agent one who has been granted the authority to act on behalf of another.

agreement of sale a written agreement between a seller and a purchaser whereby the purchaser agrees to buy a certain piece of property from the seller for a specified price.

air rights the right to use the open space above a particular property.

alienation the transfer of ownership of a property to another, either voluntarily or involuntarily.

alienation clause the clause in a mortgage or deed of trust that permits the lender to declare all unpaid principal and accrued interest due and payable if the borrower transfers title to the property.

allocated expenses costs that have been apportioned in situations where it is difficult to determine in advance how much to charge for each use of a shared supply or service. A portion may be regularly allocated to expenses such as depreciation and amortization and may be seen as a fixed cost per period, or the entire amount may be considered upfront fixed costs.

allodial system in the United States, a system of land ownership in which land is held free and clear of any rent or services due to the government; commonly contrasted with the feudal system, in which ownership is held by a monarch.

amenities features or benefits of a particular property that enhance the property's desirability and value, such as a scenic view or a pool.

amortization the method of repaying a loan or debt by making periodic installment payments composed of both principal and interest. When all principal has been repaid, it is considered fully amortized.

amortization schedule a table that shows how much of each loan payment will be applied toward principal and how much toward interest over the lifespan of the loan. It also shows the gradual decrease of the outstanding loan balance until it reaches zero.

amortize to repay a loan through regular payments that consist of principal and interest.

amortized mortgage a standard mortgage, or home loan, on which interest is calculated monthly.

annual compounding the amount of interest charged on the principal and on accumulated past interest; the formula is $P \times (1 + r) =$ annual compounding.

annualization a rate based on an entire year.

annual percentage rate (APR) the total or effective amount of interest charged on a loan, expressed as a percentage, on a yearly basis. This value is created according to a government formula intended to reflect the true annual cost of borrowing.

anti-deficiency law laws used in some states to limit the claim of a lender on default on payment of a purchase money mortgage on owner-occupied residential property to the value of the collateral.

anti-trust laws laws designed to protect free enterprise and the open marketplace by prohibiting certain business practices that restrict competition.

In reference to real estate, these laws would prevent such practices as price fixing or agreements by brokers to limit their areas of trade.

apportionments adjustment of income, expenses, or carrying charges related to real estate, usually computed to the date of closing so that the seller pays all expenses to date, then the buyer pays all expenses beginning on the closing date.

appraisal an estimate or opinion of the value of an adequately described property, as of a specific date.

appraised value an opinion of a property's fair market value, based on an appraiser's knowledge, experience, and analysis of the property, and based on comparable sales.

appraiser an individual qualified by education, training, and experience to estimate the value of real property. Appraisers may work directly for mortgage lenders, or they may be independent contractors.

appreciation an increase in the market value of a property.

appurtenance something that transfers with the title to land even if not an actual part of the property, such as an easement.

arbitration the process of settling a dispute in which the parties submit their differences to an impartial third party, on whose decision on the matter is binding.

area the surface size of a piece of property.

ARELLO the Association of Real Estate License Law Officials.

arrears an overdue debt.

assessed value the value of a property used to calculate real estate taxes.

assessment the process of assigning value on property for taxation purposes.

assessment ratio the relationship between assessed value and market value; used in determining taxes.

assessor a public official who establishes the value of a property for taxation purposes.

asset items of value owned by an individual. Assets that can be quickly converted into cash are considered "liquid assets," such as bank accounts and stock portfolios. Other assets include real estate, personal property, and debts owed.

assignment the transfer of rights or interest from one person to another.

assumption of mortgage the act of acquiring the title to a property that has an existing mortgage and agreeing to be liable for the payment of any debt still existing on that mortgage. However, the lender must accept the transfer of liability for the original borrower to be relieved of the debt.

attachment the process whereby a court takes custody of a debtor's property until the creditor's debt is satisfied.

attest to bear witness by providing a signature.

attorney-in-fact a person who is authorized under a power of attorney to act on behalf of another.

automated valuation model (AVM) computer-generated appraisals.

avulsion the removal of land from one owner to another when a stream or other body of water suddenly changes its channel.

▶ **B**

balloon mortgage a loan in which the periodic payments do not fully amortize the loan, so that a final payment (a balloon payment) is substantially larger than the amount of the periodic payments that must be made to satisfy the debt.

balloon payment the final, lump-sum payment that is due at the termination of a balloon mortgage.

bankruptcy an individual or individuals can restructure or relieve themselves of debts and liabilities by filing in federal bankruptcy court. Of the many types of bankruptcies, the most common for an individual is "Chapter 7 No Asset," which relieves the borrower of most types of debts.

bargain and sale deed a deed that conveys title but does not necessarily carry warranties against liens or encumbrances.

baseline one of the imaginary east-west lines used as a reference point when describing property with the rectangular or government survey method of property description.

basis starting point used by IRS to determine annual depreciation, amortization, and gain or loss on the sale of property.

benchmark a permanently marked point with a known elevation, used as a reference by surveyors to measure elevations.

beneficiary (1) one who benefits from the acts of another; (2) the lender in a deed of trust.

bequest personal property given by provision of a will.

betterment an improvement to property that increases its value.

bilateral contract a contract in which each party promises to perform an act in exchange for the other party's promise also to perform an act.

bill of sale a written instrument that transfers ownership of personal property. A bill of sale cannot be used to transfer ownership of real property, which is passed by deed.

binder an agreement, accompanied by an earnest money deposit, for the purchase of a piece of real estate to show the purchaser's good faith intent to complete a transaction.

biweekly mortgage a mortgage in which payments are made every two weeks instead of once a month. Therefore, instead of making 12 monthly payments during the year, the borrower makes the equivalent of 13 monthly payments. The extra payment reduces the principal, thereby reducing the time it takes to pay off a 30-year mortgage.

blanket mortgage a mortgage in which more than one parcel of real estate is pledged to cover a single debt.

blockbusting the illegal and discriminatory practice of inducing homeowners to sell their properties by suggesting or implying the introduction of members of a protected class into the neighborhood.

bona fide in good faith, honest.

bond evidence of personal debt secured by a mortgage or other lien on real estate.

boot money or property provided to make up a difference in value or equity between two properties in an exchange.

branch office a place of business secondary to a principal office. The branch office is a satellite office generally run by a licensed broker, for the benefit of the broker running the principal office, as well as the associate broker's convenience.

breach of contract violation of any conditions or terms in a contract without legal excuse.

breakeven occupancy the number of rentals required to cover all expenses on the property; thus, revenues and costs are equal and there is no profit or loss.

broker in real estate terms, it is the owner-manager of a business who brings together the parties to a real estate transaction for a fee. The roles of brokers and brokers' associates are defined by state law. In the mortgage industry, *broker* usually refers to a company or individual who does not lend the money for the loans directly, but who brokers loans to larger lenders or investors.

brokerage the business of bringing together buyers and sellers or other participants in a real estate transaction.

broker's price opinion (BPO) a broker's opinion of value based on a comparative market analysis rather than a certified appraisal.

building code local regulations that control construction, design, and materials used in construction that are based on health and safety regulations.

building line the distance from the front, rear, or sides of a building lot beyond which no structures may extend.

building restrictions limitations listed in zoning ordinances or deed restrictions on the size and type of improvements allowed on a property.

bundle of rights the concept that ownership of a property includes certain rights regarding the property, such as possession, enjoyment, control of use, and disposition.

buydown usually refers to a fixed-rate mortgage where the interest rate is "bought down" for a temporary period, usually one to three years. After that time and for the remainder of the term, the borrower's payment is calculated at the note rate. In order to buy down the initial rate for the temporary payment, a lump sum is paid and held in an account used to supplement the borrower's monthly payment. These funds usually come from the seller as a financial incentive to induce someone to buy his or her property.

buyer's broker real estate broker retained by a prospective buyer; this buyer becomes the broker's client to whom fiduciary duties are owed.

bylaws rules and regulations adopted by an association—for example, a condominium.

▶ C

cancellation clause a provision in a lease that confers on one or all parties to the lease the right to terminate the parties' obligations, should the occurrence of the condition or contingency set forth in the clause happen.

canvassing the practice of searching for prospective clients by making unsolicited phone calls and/or visiting homes door to door.

cap the limit on fluctuation rates regarding adjustable rate mortgages. Caps, or limitations, may apply to how much the loan may adjust over a six-month period, an annual period, and over the life of the loan. There is also a limit on how much that payment can change each year.

capital money used to create income, or the net worth of a business as represented by the amount by which its assets exceed its liabilities.

capital expenditure the cost of a betterment to a property.

capital gain the positive difference between the purchase and sales price of a property.

capital gains tax a tax charged on the profit gained from the sale of a capital asset.

capital improvement a permanent addition to a property, structure, or other asset that adds to the property's value.

capitalization the process of estimating the present value of an income-producing piece of property by dividing anticipated future income by a capitalization rate.

capitalization rate the rate of return a property will generate on an owner's investment.

capital loss the negative difference between the purchase and sales price of a property.

cash flow the net income produced by an investment property, calculated by deducting operating and fixed expenses from gross income.

cash flow projection an estimate of the amount of cash that is anticipated to be generated or expended over a given period of time.

caveat emptor a phrase meaning "let the buyer beware."

CC&R covenants, conditions, and restrictions of a cooperative or condominium development.

certificate of discharge a document used when the security instrument is a mortgage.

certificate of eligibility a document issued by the Veterans Administration that certifies a veteran's eligibility for a VA loan.

certificate of reasonable value (CRV) once the appraisal has been performed on a property being bought with a VA loan, the Veterans Administration issues a CRV.

certificate of sale the document given to a purchaser of real estate that is sold at a tax foreclosure sale.

certificate of title a report stating an opinion on the status of a title, based on the examination of public records.

chain of title the recorded history of conveyances and encumbrances that affect the title to a parcel of land.

chattel personal property, as opposed to real property.

chattel mortgage a loan in which personal property is pledged to secure the debt.

city a large municipality governed under a charter and granted by the state.

clear title a title that is free of liens and legal questions as to ownership of a property that is a requirement for the sale of real estate; sometimes referred to as *just title*, *good title*, or *free and clear*.

closing the point in a real estate transaction when the purchase price is paid to the seller and the deed to the property is transferred from the seller to the buyer.

closing costs there are two kinds: (1) nonrecurring closing costs and (2) prepaid items. Nonrecurring closing costs are any items paid once as a result of buying the property or obtaining a loan. Prepaid items are items that recur over time, such as property taxes and homeowners insurance. A lender makes an attempt to estimate the amount of nonrecurring closing costs and prepaid items on the good faith estimate, which is issued to the borrower within three days of receiving a home loan application.

closing date the date on which the buyer takes over the property.

closing statement a written account of funds received and disbursed during a real estate transaction. The buyer and seller receive separate closing statements.

cloud on the title an outstanding claim or encumbrance that can affect or impair the owner's title.

clustering the grouping of home sites within a subdivision on smaller lots than normal, with the remaining land slated for use as common areas.

codicil a supplement or addition to a will that modifies the original instrument.

coinsurance clause a clause in an insurance policy that requires the insured to pay a portion of any loss experienced.

collateral something of value hypothecated (real property) or pledged (personal property) by a borrower as security for a debt.

collection when a borrower falls behind, the lender contacts the borrower in an effort to bring the loan current. The loan goes to "collection."

color of title an instrument that gives evidence of title, but may not be legally adequate to actually convey title.

commercial property property used to produce income, such as an office building or a restaurant.

commingling the illegal act of an agent mixing a client's monies, which should be held in a separate escrow account, with the agent's personal monies; in some states, it means placing funds that are separate property in an account containing funds that are community property.

commission the fee paid to a broker for services rendered in a real estate transaction.

commitment letter a pledge in writing affirming an agreement.

common areas portions of a building, land, and amenities owned (or managed) by a planned unit development or condominium project's home-owners association or a cooperative project's cooperative corporation. These areas are used by all of the unit owners, who share in the common expenses of their operation and maintenance. Common areas may include swimming pools, tennis courts, and other recreational facilities, as well as common corridors of buildings, parking areas, and lobbies.

common denominator a number that all of the bottom numbers in a group of fractions may be divided evenly; allows for the addition and subtraction of fractions.

common law the body of laws derived from local custom and judicial precedent.

community property a system of property ownership in which each spouse has equal interest in property acquired during the marriage; recognized in nine states.

comparable sales recent sales of similar properties in nearby areas that are used to help estimate the current market value of a property.

comparative market analysis (CMA) an analysis of market value used to determine a probable selling price using recently sold properties most like the subject property.

competent parties people who are legally qualified to enter a contract, usually meaning that they are of legal age, of sound mind, and not under the influence of drugs or other mind-altering substances.

competitive market analysis (CMA) an analysis of market value used to assist a seller in determining an asking price, using currently active listings, expired listings, and sold properties comparable to the subject property.

compound growth rate year-over-year growth rate of an investment over a specified period of time.

compound interest money on principal plus any interest reinvested.

condemnation the judicial process by which the government exercises its power of eminent domain.

condominium a form of ownership in which an individual owns a specific unit in a multiunit building and shares ownership of common areas with other unit owners.

condominium conversion changing the ownership of an existing building (usually a multi-dwelling rental unit) from single ownership to condominium ownership.

conformity an appraisal principle that asserts that property achieves its maximum value when a neighborhood is homogeneous in its use of land; the basis for zoning ordinances.

consideration something of value that induces parties to enter into a contract, such as money or services.

construction mortgage a short-term loan used to finance the building of improvements to real estate.

constructive eviction action or inaction by a landlord that renders a property uninhabitable, forcing a tenant to move out with no further liability for rent.

constructive notice notice of a fact given by making the fact part of the public record. All persons are responsible for knowing the information, whether or not they have actually seen the record.

contingency a condition that must be met before a contract is legally binding. A satisfactory home inspection report from a qualified home inspector is an example of a common type of contingency.

contract an agreement between two or more legally competent parties to do or to refrain from doing some legal act in exchange for a consideration.

contract for deed a contract for the sale of a parcel of real estate in which the buyer makes periodic payments to the seller and receives the title to the property only after all, or a substantial part, of the purchase price has been paid, or regular payments have been made for one year or longer.

contract rate the interest rate specified in the loan agreement.

conventional loan a loan that is neither insured nor guaranteed by an agency of government.

conversion option an option in an adjustable-rate mortgage to convert it to a fixed-rate mortgage.

convertible ARM an adjustable-rate mortgage that allows the borrower to change the ARM to a fixed-rate mortgage at a specific time.

conveyance the transfer of title from the grantor to the grantee.

cooperative a form of property ownership in which a corporation owns a multiunit building and stockholders of the corporation may lease and occupy individual units of the building through a proprietary lease.

corporation a legal entity with potentially perpetual existence that is created and owned by shareholders who appoint a board of directors to direct the business affairs of the corporation.

cost approach an appraisal method whereby the value of a property is calculated by estimating the cost of constructing a comparable building, subtracting depreciation, and adding land value.

cost method an accounting method whereby the value of a group of assets or expenses is assumed to be equal to the average cost of the assets or expenses in the group.

counteroffer an offer submitted in response to an offer. It has the effect of overriding the original offer.

covenant an agreement or promise between parties to do or not do specific acts.

covenant of seisin the seller of real estate promises he or she has rightful title and is delivering that title to the buyer.

credit an agreement in which a borrower receives something of value in exchange for a promise to repay the lender.

credit history a record of an individual's repayment of debt.

cul-de-sac a dead-end street that widens at the end, creating a circular turnaround area.

curtesy the statutory or common law right of a husband to all or part of real estate owned by his deceased wife, regardless of will provisions, recognized in some states.

curtilage area of land occupied by a building, its outbuildings, and yard, either actually enclosed or considered enclosed.

▶ D

damages the amount of money recoverable by a person who has been injured by the actions of another.

datum a specific point used in surveying.

DBA the abbreviation for "doing business as."

debt an amount owed to another.

debt coverage ratio (DCR) a measure of an income-producing property's ability to cover the monthly mortgage payments.

debt service the amount of money needed to make payments of principal and interest on a loan.

decedent a person who dies.

decimal equivalence the concept that a number in decimal form equals a number in fraction form.

declining balance depreciation a common depreciation-calculation system that expenses the asset at a constant rate, which results in declining depreciation charges each successive period.

dedication the donation of private property by its owner to a governmental body for public use.

deed a written document that, when properly signed and delivered, conveys title to real property from the grantor to the grantee.

deed-in-lieu a foreclosure instrument used to convey title to the lender when the borrower is in default and wants to avoid foreclosure.

deed of trust (trust deed) a deed in which the title to property is transferred to a third-party trustee to secure repayment of a loan; three-party mortgage arrangement.

deed restriction an imposed restriction for the purpose of limiting the use of land, such as the size or type of improvements to be allowed. Also called a *restrictive covenant*.

default the failure to perform a contractual duty.

defeasance clause a clause in a mortgage that renders the mortgage void where all obligations have been fulfilled.

deficiency judgment a personal claim against a borrower when mortgaged property is foreclosed and sale of the property does not produce sufficient funds to pay off the mortgage. Deficiency judgments may be prohibited in some circumstances by anti-deficiency protection.

delinquency failure to make mortgage or loan payments when payments are due.

density zoning a zoning ordinance that restricts the number of houses or dwelling units that can be built per acre in a particular area, such as a subdivision.

depreciation a loss in value because of physical deterioration or functional or external obsolescence.

descent the transfer of property to an owner's heirs when the owner dies intestate.

devise the transfer of title to real estate by will.

devisee one who receives a bequest of real estate by will.

devisor one who grants real estate by will.

directional growth the direction toward which certain residential sections of a city are expected to grow.

discount a decrease in the amount of a loan.

discounted cash flow (DCF) the estimated present value of future cash.

discount point one percent of the loan amount charged by a lender at closing to increase a loan's effective yield and lower the fare rate to the borrower.

discount rate the rate that lenders pay for mortgage funds—a higher rate is passed on to the borrower.

dispossess to remove a tenant from property by legal process.

documentary stamp tax notes the transfer tax that some states levy on mortgages; a revenue stamp is affixed to documents transferring title to real property.

dominant estate (tenement) property that includes the right to use an easement on adjoining property.

dower the right of a widow in the property of her husband upon his death in noncommunity property states.

down payment the part of the purchase price that the buyer pays in cash and is not financed with a mortgage or loan.

dual agency an agent who represents both parties in a transaction.

due-on-sale clause a provision in a mortgage that allows the lender to demand repayment in full if the borrower sells the property that serves as security for the mortgage.

duress the use of unlawful means to force a person to act or to refrain from an action against his or her will.

▶ E

earnest money down payment made by a buyer of real estate as evidence of good faith.

easement the right of one party to use the land of another for a particular purpose, such as to lay utility lines.

easement by necessity an easement, granted by law and requiring court action that is deemed necessary for the full enjoyment of a parcel of land. An example would be an easement allowing access from landlocked property to a road.

easement by prescription a means of acquiring an easement by continued, open, and hostile use of someone else's property for a statutorily defined period of time.

easement in gross a personal right granted by an owner with no requirement that the easement holder own adjoining land.

economic life the period of time over which an improved property will generate sufficient income to justify its continued existence.

economic rent a return above the opportunity cost of an asset or service.

effective age an appraiser's estimate of the physical condition of a building. The actual age of a building may be different than its effective age.

effective gross income in relation to income-producing property, gross income minus a vacancy allowance and collection loss plus miscellaneous income equals effective gross income.

effective interest rate the yield on debt, such as a mortgage, based on the purchase price.

effective tax rate the amount of tax paid divided by the net taxable income.

emblements cultivated crops; generally considered to be personal property.

eminent domain the right of a government to take private property for public use upon payment of its fair market value. Eminent domain is the basis for condemnation proceedings.

encroachment a trespass caused when a structure, such as a wall or fence, invades another person's land or airspace.

encumbrance anything that affects or limits the title to a property, such as easements, leases, mortgages, or restrictions.

equation a mathematical statement that demonstrates the equality of two expressions that are separated into left and right sides by an equal sign.

equitable title the interest in a piece of real estate held by a buyer who has agreed to purchase the property, but has not yet completed the transaction; the interest of a buyer under a contract for deed.

equity the difference between the current market value of a property and the outstanding indebtedness due on it.

equity of redemption the right of a borrower to stop the foreclosure process.

equity-to-value ratio the amount of principal paid in relation to the present value of the property; the amount received when the property is sold.

erosion the gradual wearing away of land by wind, water, and other natural processes.

escalation clause a clause in a lease allowing the lessor to charge more rent based on an increase in costs; sometimes called a pass-through clause.

escheat the claim to property by the state when the owner dies intestate and no heirs can be found.

escrow the deposit of funds and/or documents with a disinterested third party for safekeeping until the terms of the escrow agreement have been met.

escrow account a trust account established to hold escrow funds for safe-keeping until disbursement.

escrow analysis annual report to disclose escrow receipts, payments, and current balances.

escrow disbursements money paid from an escrow account.

estate an interest in real property. The sum total of all the real property and personal property owned by an individual.

estate for years a leasehold estate granting possession for a definite period of time.

estate tax federal tax levied on property transferred upon death.

estoppel certificate a document that certifies the outstanding amount owed on a mortgage loan, as well as the rate of interest.

et al. abbreviation for the Latin phrase *et alius*, meaning "and another."

et ux. abbreviation for Latin term *et uxor*, meaning "and wife."

et vir Latin term meaning "and husband."

eviction the lawful expulsion of an occupant from real property.

evidence of title a document that identifies ownership of property.

examination of title a review of an abstract to determine current condition of title.

exchange a transaction in which property is traded for another property, rather than sold for money or other consideration.

exclusive agency listing a contract between a property owner and one broker that only gives the broker the right to sell the property for a fee within a specified period of time but does not obligate the owner to pay the broker a fee if the owner produces his or her own buyer without the broker's assistance. The owner is barred only from appointing another broker within this time period.

exclusive right to sell a contract between a property owner and a broker that gives the broker the right to collect a commission regardless of who sells the property during the specified period of time of the agreement.

exculpatory clause a statement that absolves or waives a right or obligation.

execution the signing of a contract.

executor/executrix a person named in a will to administer an estate. The court will appoint an administrator if no executor is named. *Executrix* is the feminine form.

executory contract a contract in which one or more of the obligations have yet to be performed.

executed contract a contract in which all obligations have been fully performed.

expected return an estimate of the value of an investment, based on the average of a probability distribution of possible returns.

express contract an oral or written contract in which the terms are expressed in words.

extension agreement an agreement between mortgagor and mortgagee to extend the maturity date of the mortgage after it is due.

external obsolescence a loss in value of a property because of factors outside the property, such as a change in surrounding land use.

▶ F

fair housing law a term used to refer to federal and state laws prohibiting discrimination in the sale or rental of residential property.

fair market value the highest price that a buyer, willing but not compelled to buy, would pay, and the lowest a seller, willing but not compelled to sell, would accept.

Federal Housing Administration (FHA) an agency within the U.S. Department of Housing and Urban Development (HUD) that insures mortgage loans by FHA-approved lenders to make loans available to buyers with limited cash.

Federal National Mortgage Association (Fannie Mae) a privately owned corporation that buys existing government-backed and conventional mortgages.

Federal Reserve System the central banking system of the United States that controls the monetary policy and, therefore, the money supply, interest rates, and availability of credit.

fee simple the most complete form of ownership of real estate.

FHA-insured loan a loan insured by the Federal Housing Administration.

fiduciary relationship a legal relationship with an obligation of trust, as that of agent and principal.

financial calculator a device or computer program that performs mathematical functions relating to finance.

finder's fee a fee or commission paid to a mortgage broker for finding a mortgage loan for a prospective borrower.

first mortgage a mortgage that has priority to be satisfied over all other mortgages.

fixed-rate loan a loan with an interest rate that does not change during the entire term of the loan.

fixture an article of personal property that has been permanently attached to the real estate so as to become an integral part of the real estate.

floor see *interest rate floor*.

foreclosure the legal process by which a borrower in default of a mortgage is deprived of interest in the mortgaged property. Usually, this involves a forced sale of the property at public auction, where the proceeds of the sale are applied to the mortgage debt.

forfeiture the loss of money, property, rights, or privileges because of a breach of legal obligation.

forward rate the price of an asset at some point in the future.

fraction an expression of the relationship between two numbers; the numerator indicates the number of equal parts, and the denominator names the total number of parts in the whole.

franchise in real estate, an organization that lends a standardized trade name, operating procedures, referral services, and supplies to member brokerages.

fraud a deliberate misstatement of material fact or an act or omission made with deliberate intent to deceive (active fraud) or gross disregard for the truth (constructive fraud).

freehold estate an estate of ownership in real property.

front foot a measurement of property taken by measuring the frontage of the property along the street line.

functional obsolescence a loss in value of a property due to causes within the property, such as faulty design, outdated structural style, or inadequacy to function properly.

future interest ownership interest in property that cannot be enjoyed until the occurrence of some event; sometimes referred to as a household or equitable interest.

future value (FV) a measure of what an amount of money would be worth at a specified time in the future assuming a certain interest rate, without adjustment for inflation or other factors that may affect the money's value.

▶ G

general agent an agent who is authorized to act for and obligate a principal in a specific range of matters, as specified by their mutual agreement.

general lien a claim on all property, real and personal, owned by a debtor.

general warranty deed an instrument in which the grantor guarantees the grantee that the title being conveyed is good and free of other claims or encumbrances.

government-backed mortgage a mortgage that is insured by the Federal Housing Administration (FHA) or guaranteed by the Department of Veterans Affairs (VA) or the Rural Housing Service (RHS). Mortgages that are not government loans are identified as conventional loans.

Government National Mortgage Association (Ginnie Mae) a government-owned corporation within the U.S. Department of Housing and Urban Development (HUD). Ginnie Mae manages and liquidates government-backed loans and assists HUD in special lending projects.

government survey system a method of land description in which meridians (lines of longitude) and baselines (lines of latitude) are used to divide land into townships and sections.

graduated lease a lease that calls for periodic, stated changes in rent during the term of the lease.

grant the transfer of title to real property by deed.

grant deed a deed that includes three warranties: (1) that the owner has the right to convey title to the property, (2) that there are no encumbrances other than those noted specifically in the deed, and (3) that the owner will convey any future interest that he or she may acquire in the property.

grantee one who receives title to real property.

grantor one who conveys title to real property; the present owner.

gross income the total income received from a property before deducting expenses.

gross income multiplier a rough method of estimating the market value of an income property by multiplying its gross annual rent by a multiplier discovered by dividing the sales price of comparable properties by their annual gross rent.

gross lease a lease in which a tenant pays only a fixed amount for rental and the landlord pays all operating expenses and taxes.

gross operating income (GOI) gross potential operating income (if fully rented and rent is paid in full) less vacancy and credit loss.

gross rent multiplier similar to *gross income multiplier,* except that it looks at the relationship between sales price and monthly gross rent.

ground lease a lease of land only, on which a tenant already owns a building or will construct improvements.

growth rate the compounded annualized rate at which money increases.

guaranteed sale plan an agreement between a broker and a seller that the broker will buy the seller's property if it does not sell within a specified period of time.

guardian one who is legally responsible for the care of another person's rights and/or property.

▶ **H**

habendum **clause** the clause in a deed, beginning with the words "to have and to hold," that defines or limits the exact interest in the estate granted by the deed.

half-year convention the assumption when calculating depreciation for non-real estate property that the property began to be used in mid-year.

hamlet a small village.

heir one who is legally entitled to receive property when the owner dies intestate.

hereditament any type of inheritable property both real and personal.

highest and best use the legally permitted use of a parcel of land that will yield the greatest return to the owner in terms of money or amenities.

holding period the length of time an asset is held; affects whether a gain or loss is long or short term.

holdover tenancy a tenancy where a lessee retains possession of the property after the lease has expired, and the landlord, by continuing to accept rent, agrees to the tenant's continued occupancy.

holographic will a will that is entirely handwritten, dated, and signed by the testator.

home equity conversion mortgage (HECM) often called a reverse-annuity mortgage; instead of making payments to a lender, the lender makes payments to you. It enables older homeowners to convert the equity they have in their homes into cash, usually in the form of monthly payments. Unlike traditional home equity loans, a borrower does not qualify on the basis of income but on the value of his or her home. In addition, the loan does not have to be repaid until the borrower no longer occupies the property.

home equity line of credit a mortgage loan that allows the borrower to obtain cash drawn against the equity of his or her home, up to a predetermined amount.

home inspection a thorough inspection by a professional that evaluates the structural and mechanical condition of a property. A satisfactory home inspection is often included as a contingency by the purchaser.

homeowners insurance an insurance policy specifically designed to protect residential property owners against financial loss from common risks such as fire, theft, and liability.

homeowners warranty an insurance policy that protects purchasers of newly constructed or pre-owned homes against certain structural and mechanical defects.

homestead the parcel of land and improvements legally qualifying as the owner's principal residence.

homestead exemption where available, a means to reduce the assessed value of a primary residence for the purposes of calculating property tax.

HUD an acronym for the Department of Housing and Urban Development, a federal agency that enforces federal fair housing laws and oversees agencies such as FHA and GNMA.

hypothecate the act of pledging property as collateral for a loan without giving up possession of the pledged property.

▶ I

illiquidity an asset that is difficult to convert into cash.

implied contract a contract whereby the agreement of the parties is created by their conduct.

improvement human-made addition to real estate.

income capitalization approach a method of estimating the value of income-producing property by dividing its expected annual net operating income of the property by a capitalization rate.

income method an approach used to appraise income properties in order to calculate the property's current value; based on the net income generated by the property.

income property real estate developed or improved to produce income.

income rate value (IRV) income divided by rate equals value, known as a CAP rate, the amount of money an investor has to earn in order to invest in a property.

incorporeal right intangible, non-possessory rights in real estate, such as an easement or right of way.

indemnify to hold harmless and to reimburse or compensate someone for a loss.

independent contractor one who is retained by another to perform a certain task and is not subject to the control and direction of the hiring person with regard to the end result of the task. Individual contractors receive a fee for their services but pay their own expenses and taxes and receive no employee benefits.

index a number used to compute the interest rate for an adjustable-rate mortgage (ARM). The index is a published number or percentage, such as the average yield on Treasury bills. A margin is added to the index to determine the interest rate to be charged on the ARM. This interest rate is subject to any caps that are associated with the mortgage.

industrial property buildings and land used for the manufacture and distribution of goods, such as a factory.

inflation an increase in the amount of money or credit available in relation to the amount of goods or services available, which causes an increase in the general price level of goods and services.

initial interest rate the beginning interest rate of the mortgage at the time of closing. This rate changes for an adjustable-rate mortgage (ARM).

installment the regular, periodic payment that a borrower agrees to make to a lender, usually related to a loan.

installment contract see *contract for deed*.

installment loan borrowed money that is repaid in periodic payments, known as installments.

installment sale a transaction in which the sales price is paid to the seller in two or more installments over more than one calendar year.

insurance a contract that provides indemnification from specific losses in exchange for a periodic payment. The individual contract is known as an insurance policy, and the periodic payment is known as an insurance premium.

insurance binder a document that states that temporary insurance is in effect until a permanent insurance policy is issued.

insured mortgage a mortgage that is protected by the Federal Housing Administration (FHA) or by private mortgage insurance (PMI). If the borrower defaults on the loan, the insurer must pay the lender the insured amount.

intangible tax a one-time tax imposed on personal property, in some states on a mortgage.

interest a fee charged by a lender for the use of the money loaned; or a share of ownership in real estate.

interest accrual rate the percentage rate at which interest accrues on the mortgage.

interest rate the rent or rate charged to use funds belonging to another.

interest rate buydown plan an arrangement in which the property seller (or any other party) deposits money into an account so that it can be released each month to reduce the mortgagor's monthly payments during the early years of a mortgage. During the specified period, the mortgagor's effective interest rate is "bought down" below the actual interest rate.

interest rate ceiling the maximum interest rate that may be charged for an adjustable-rate mortgage (ARM), as specified in the mortgage note.

interest rate floor the minimum interest rate for an adjustable-rate mortgage (ARM), as specified in the mortgage note.

interest rate risk the risk that changes in market rates will adversely affect profitability and capital.

interim financing a short-term loan made during the building phase of a project; also known as a construction loan.

intestate to die without having authored a valid will.

invalid not legally binding or enforceable.

inventory the number of months it would take to sell the total number of homes available for sale at any given time at the current sales pace.

investment property a property not occupied by the owner.

investment risk the potential difference between forecasted future value; can also be associated with other variables such as rent, vacancy, operating expenses, etc.

▶ **J**

joint tenancy co-ownership that gives each tenant equal interest and equal rights in the property, including the right of survivorship.

joint venture an agreement between two or more parties to engage in a specific business enterprise.

judgment a decision rendered by court determining the rights and obligations of parties to an action or lawsuit.

judgment lien a lien on the property of a debtor resulting from a court judgment.

judicial foreclosure a proceeding that is handled as a civil lawsuit and conducted through court; used in some states.

jumbo loan a loan that exceeds Fannie Mae's mortgage amount limits. Also called a *non-conforming loan*.

junior mortgage any mortgage that is inferior to a first lien and that will be satisfied only after the first mortgage; also called a *secondary mortgage*.

▶ **L**

laches a doctrine used by a court to bar the assertion of a legal claim or right, based on the failure to assert the claim in a timely manner.

land the earth from its surface to its center, and the airspace above it.

landlocked property surrounded on all sides by property belonging to another.

lease a contract between a landlord and a tenant wherein the landlord grants the tenant possession and use of the property for a specified period of time and for a consideration.

leased fee the landlord's interest in a parcel of leased property.

lease option a financing option that allows homebuyers to lease a home with an option to buy. Each month's rent payment may consist of rent, plus an additional amount that can be applied toward the down payment on an already specified price.

leasehold a tenant's right to occupy a parcel of real estate for the term of a lease.

legal description a description of a parcel of real estate specific and complete enough for an independent surveyor to locate and identify it.

lessee the one who receives that right to use and occupy the property during the term of the leasehold estate.

lessor the owner of the property who grants the right of possession to the lessee.

leverage the use of borrowed funds to purchase an asset.

levy to assess or collect a tax.

license (1) a revocable authorization to perform a particular act on another's property; (2) authorization granted by a state to act as a real estate broker or salesperson.

lien a legal claim against a property to secure payment of a financial obligation.

life estate a freehold estate in real property limited in duration to the lifetime of the holder of the life estate or another specified person.

life tenant one who holds a life estate.

like-kind exchange (1031 exchange) a way to structure the sale of property so that the tax on the profit is deferred; the property that is sold is replaced with another "like kind" property.

liquidity the ability to convert an asset into cash.

lis pendens a Latin phrase meaning "suit pending"; a public notice that a lawsuit has been filed that may affect the title to a particular piece of property.

listing agreement a contract between the owner and a licensed real estate broker wherein the broker is employed to sell real estate on the owner's terms within a given time, for which service the owner agrees to pay the broker an agreed-upon fee.

listing broker a broker who contracts with a property owner to sell or lease the described property; the listing agreement typically may provide for the broker to make property available through a multiple-listing system.

littoral rights landowner's claim to use water in large, navigable lakes and oceans adjacent to property; ownership rights to land-bordering bodies of water up to the high-water mark.

loan a sum of borrowed money, or principal, that is generally repaid with interest.

loan officer also known as a lender; serves several functions and has various responsibilities, such as soliciting loans; a loan officer both represents the lending institution and represents the borrower to the lending institution.

loan-to-value ratio the value of your property compared to the amount of a loan; calculated by dividing the loan amount by the value of the property or the selling/purchase price, whichever is lower.

lock in an agreement in which the lender guarantees a specified interest rate for a certain amount of time.

lock-in period the time period during which the lender has guaranteed an interest rate to a borrower.

lot and block description a method of describing a particular property by referring to a lot and block number within a subdivision recorded in the public record.

lot size the dimensions, or area, of a piece of property.

► **M**

management agreement a contract between the owner of an income property and a firm or individual who agrees to manage the property.

margin the difference between the interest rate and the index on an adjustable-rate mortgage. The margin remains stable over the life of the loan, while the index fluctuates.

margin of profit a measure of profitability calculated by dividing net income by net sales revenue, expressed as a percentage.

market data approach a method of estimating the value of a property by comparing it to similar properties recently sold and making monetary adjustments for the differences between the subject property and the comparable property.

market risk the chance that the value of an investment will decrease because of changes in market factors that affect the entire asset class.

market value the amount that a seller may expect to obtain for merchandise, services, or securities in the open market.

marketable title title to property that is free from encumbrances and reasonable doubts and that a court would compel a buyer to accept.

measurements and boundaries see *metes and bounds*.

mechanic's lien a statutory lien created to secure payment for those who supply labor or materials for the construction of an improvement to land.

metes and bounds a method of describing a parcel of land using direction and distance.

mid-month convention the assumption when calculating depreciation for residential real estate that the property began to be used in the middle of the month.

mill one-tenth of one cent; used by some states to express or calculate property tax rates.

minor a person who has not attained the legal age of majority.

misrepresentation a misstatement of fact, either deliberate or unintentional.

mixed number a combination of a whole number followed by a proper fraction.

modification the act of changing any of the terms of the mortgage.

Modified Accelerated Cost Recovery System (MACRS) a system used to calculate depreciation on properties after 1987.

money judgment a court order to settle a claim with a monetary payment, rather than specific performance.

monthly compounding the interest paid both on the original principal and on the accumulated past interest.

month-to-month tenancy tenancy in which the tenant rents for only one month at a time.

monument a fixed, visible marker used to establish boundaries for a survey.

mortgage a written instrument that pledges property to secure payment of a debt obligation as evidenced by a promissory note. When duly recorded in the public record, a mortgage creates a lien against the title to a property.

mortgage banker an entity that originates, funds, and services loans to be sold into the secondary money market.

mortgage broker an entity that, for a fee, brings borrowers together with lenders.

mortgage lien an encumbrance created by recording a mortgage.

mortgagee the lender who benefits from the mortgage.

mortgage registration tax a transfer tax; an amount paid for recording a mortgage.

mortgagor the borrower who pledges the property as collateral.

multi-dwelling units properties that provide separate housing units for more than one family that secure only a single mortgage. Apartment buildings are also considered multi-dwelling units.

multiple-listing system (MLS—also multiple-listing service) the method of marketing a property listing to all participants in the MLS.

mutual rescission an agreement by all parties to a contract to release one another from the obligations of the contract.

► N

negative amortization occurs when an adjustable rate mortgage is allowed to fluctuate independently of a required minimum payment. A gradual increase in mortgage debt happens when the monthly payment is not large enough to cover the entire principal and interest due. The amount of the shortfall is added to the remaining balance to create negative amortization.

negative cash flow a situation in which more cash is being spent than is being earned.

net breakeven point the occupancy level needed to pay for operating expenses and debt service, but leaving no cash flow.

net income the income produced by a property, calculated by deducting operating expenses from gross income.

net lease a lease that requires the tenant to pay maintenance and operating expenses, as well as rent.

net listing a listing in which the broker's fee is established as anything above a specified amount to be received by the seller from the sale of the property.

net operating income (NOI) gross income minus all operating expenses except income taxes and financing expenses.

net present value (NPV) current value of cash inflows minus the current value of cash outflows; used to analyze the profitability of an investment or project.

net proceeds the amount of money received from a sale minus transaction costs.

net worth the value of all of a person's assets.

no cash-out refinance a refinance transaction in which the new mortgage amount is limited to the sum of the remaining balance of the existing first mortgage.

nominal rate an annual rate that equals the interest rate per compounding period multiplied by the number of compounding periods.

non-conforming use a use of land that is permitted to continue, or grandfathered, even after a zoning ordinance is passed that prohibits the use.

nonliquid asset an asset that cannot easily be converted into cash.

notarize to attest or certify by a notary public.

notary public a person who is authorized to administer oaths and take acknowledgments.

note a written instrument acknowledging a debt, with a promise to repay, including an outline of the terms of repayment.

note rate the interest rate on a promissory note.

notice of default a formal written notice to a borrower that a default has occurred on a loan and that legal action may be taken.

novation the substitution of a new contract for an existing one; the new contract must reference the first and indicate that the first is being replaced and no longer has any force and effect.

▶ **O**

obligee a person on whose favor an obligation is entered.

obligor a person who is bound to another by an obligation.

obsolescence a loss in the value of a property because of functional or external factors.

occupancy rate the percentage of currently occupied units.

offer to propose as payment; to bid on property.

offer and acceptance two necessary elements for the creation of a contract.

open-end mortgage a loan containing a clause that allows the mortgagor to borrow additional funds from the lender, up to a specified amount, without rewriting the mortgage.

open listing a listing contract given to one or more brokers in which a commission is paid only to the broker who procures a sale. If the owner sells the house without the assistance of one of the brokers, no commission is due.

operating cash flow earnings before interest and taxes plus depreciation minus taxes; the amount of cash generated from the revenues a company brings in, excluding costs associated with long-term investment on capital items or investment in securities.

operating expense a normal business expense.

operating expense ratio a relationship showing operating expenses divided by potential gross income.

opinion of title an opinion, usually given by an attorney, regarding the status of a title to property.

option an agreement that gives a prospective buyer the right to purchase a seller's property within a specified period of time for a specified price.

optionee one who receives or holds an option.

optionor one who grants an option; the property owner.

ordinance a municipal regulation.

original principal balance the total amount of principal owed on a loan before any payments are made; the amount borrowed.

origination fee the amount charged by a lender to cover the cost of assembling the loan package and originating the loan.

owner financing a real estate transaction in which the property seller provides all or part of the financing.

ownership the exclusive right to use, possess, control, and dispose of property.

▶ **P**

package mortgage a mortgage that pledges both real and personal property as collateral to secure repayment of a loan.

parcel a lot or specific portion of a large tract of real estate.

participation mortgage a type of mortgage in which the lender receives a certain percentage of the income or resale proceeds from a property, as well as interest on the loan.

partition the division of property held by co-owners into individual shares.

partnership an agreement between two parties to conduct business for profit. In a partnership, property is owned by the partnership, not the individual partners, so partners cannot sell their interest in the property without the consent of the other partners.

party wall a common wall used to separate two adjoining properties.

payee one who receives payment from another.

payment cap on an adjustable rate mortgage, a limit on the maximum monthly payment that can be charged during the life of the mortgage; does not affect interest and, therefore, negatively affects amortization.

payment to amortize an additional amount paid each month to be applied to the principal balance.

payor one who makes payment to another.

percent/percentage one part out of 100.

percentage lease a lease in which the rental rate is based on a percentage of the tenant's gross sales. This type of lease is most often used for retail space.

percentage rent a lease that provides the tenant with lower base rent in return for paying the landlord a higher percentage of sales.

per front foot a measurement along the front property.

perimeter the sum of the lengths of all sides of an object.

periodic estate tenancy that automatically renews itself until either the landlord or tenant gives notice to terminate it.

personal property (hereditaments) all items that are not permanently attached to real estate; also known as chattels.

physical deterioration a loss in the value of a property because of impairment of its physical condition.

PITI principal, interest, taxes, and insurance—the components of a regular mortgage payment.

planned unit development (PUD) a type of zoning that provides for residential and commercial uses within a specified area.

plat a map of subdivided land showing the boundaries of individual parcels or lots.

plat book a group of maps located in the public record showing the division of land into subdivisions, blocks, and individual parcels or lots.

plat number a number that identifies a parcel of real estate for which a plat has been recorded in the public record.

plottage combining two or more parcels of real estate resulting in increased usage and value.

PMI private mortgage insurance.

point a point is one percent of the loan.

point of beginning the starting point for a survey using the metes and bounds method of description.

police power the right of the government to enact laws, ordinances, and regulations to protect the public health, safety, welfare, and morals.

positive cash flow a situation in which the long-term cash coming in exceeds the long-term cash going out; the formula is that the loan-to-value ratio multiplied by the annual constant must be lower than the CAP rate to get positive cash flow.

potential gross income (PGI) the amount of income that could be produced by a real property, assuming no vacancies or collection losses.

power of attorney a legal document that authorizes someone to act on another's behalf. A power of attorney can grant complete authority or can be limited to certain acts and/or certain periods of time.

preapproval condition where a borrower has completed a loan application and provided debt, income, and savings documentation that an underwriter has reviewed and approved. A preapproval is usually done at a certain loan amount, making assumptions about what the interest rate will actually be at the time the loan is actually made, as well as estimates for the amount that will be paid for property taxes, insurance, and so on.

prepaid expense an asset on a balance sheet as a result of paying in advance for goods and services to be received in the near future.

prepaid interest the money paid at closing to cover the period from the time the mortgage is funded to the date the first payment is due.

prepayment amount paid to reduce the outstanding principal balance of a loan before the due date.

prepayment penalty a fee charged to a borrower by a lender for paying off a debt before the term of the loan expires.

prequalification a lender's opinion on the ability of a borrower to qualify for a loan, based on furnished information regarding debt, income, and available capital for down payment, closing costs, and prepaids. Prequalification is less formal than preapproval.

prescription a method of acquiring an easement to property by prolonged, unauthorized use.

present value (PV) the amount that a future sum of money is worth today given a specified rate of return.

pretax cash flow earnings before amortization and depreciation and tax payments; also known as "before-tax cash flow."

primary mortgage market the financial market in which loans are originated, funded, and serviced.

prime rate the short-term interest rate that banks charge to their preferred customers. Changes in prime rate are used as the indexes in some adjustable-rate mortgages, such as home equity lines of credit.

principal (1) one who authorizes another to act on his or her behalf; (2) one of the contracting parties to a transaction; (3) the amount of money borrowed in a loan, separate from the interest charged on it.

principal balance the balance of principal on a mortgage, exclusive of interest or other charges.

principal meridian one of the 36 longitudinal lines used in the rectangular survey system method of land description.

principal plus interest (P + I) the ratio of net revenues to the debt service requirements.

probate the judicial procedure of proving the validity of a will.

procuring cause the action that brings about the desired result. For example, if a broker takes actions that result in a sale, the broker is the procuring cause of the sale.

profitability the rate of profit on an investment; similar to the rate of return on an investment.

promissory note a document that details the terms of the loan and is the debt instrument.

property management the operating of an income property for another.

property tax a tax levied by the government on property, real or personal.

prorate to divide ongoing property costs such as taxes or maintenance fees proportionately between buyer and seller at closing.

pur autre vie a phrase meaning "for the life of another." In a life estate *pur autre vie*, the term of the estate is measured by the life of a person other than the person who holds the life estate.

purchase agreement a written contract signed by the buyer and seller stating the terms and conditions under which a property will be sold.

purchase money mortgage a mortgage given by a buyer to a seller to secure repayment of any loan used to pay part or all of the purchase price.

purchase price the monetary amount a buyer pays for a property.

▶ **Q**

qualifying ratios calculations to determine whether a borrower can qualify for a mortgage. There are two ratios. The "top" ratio is a calculation of the borrower's monthly housing costs (principle, taxes, insurance, mortgage insurance, homeowners association fees) as a percentage of monthly income. The "bottom" ratio includes housing costs as well as all other monthly debt.

quitclaim deed a conveyance whereby the grantor transfers without warranty or obligations whatever interest or title he or she may have.

▶ **R**

range an area of land six miles wide, numbered east or west from a principal meridian in the rectangular survey system.

rate of interest a rate charged or paid for the use of money; calculated by dividing the amount of interest by the amount of principal.

ready, willing, and able description of someone who is able to pay the asking price for a property and is prepared to complete the transaction.

real estate land, the earth below it, the air above it, and anything permanently attached to it.

real estate agent a real estate broker who has been appointed to market a property for and represent the property owner (listing agent); or a broker who has been appointed to represent the interest of the buyer (buyer's agent).

real estate board an organization whose members consist primarily of real estate sales agents, brokers, and administrators.

real estate broker a licensed person, association, partnership, or corporation who negotiates real estate transactions for others for a fee.

Real Estate Settlement Procedures Act (RESPA) a consumer protection law that requires lenders to give borrowers advance notice of closing costs and prohibits certain abusive practices against buyers using federally related loans to purchase their homes.

real property the rights of ownership to land and its improvements.

real rate of return the annual percentage return on an investment, adjusted for changes in prices because of inflation or deflation.

REALTOR® a registered trademark for use by members of the National Association of REALTORS® and affiliated state and local associations.

recapture a right, stipulated by the seller of an asset, to purchase back some or all of the assets within a certain period of time.

reconciliation in appraisal, the method of considering various approaches in order to determine the final estimate of the value of the property being appraised.

recording entering documents, such as deeds and mortgages, into the public record to give constructive notice.

recovery period the allowable length of time to depreciate residential rental property for which 80% or more of the gross rental income for the tax year is from dwelling units.

rectangular survey system a method of land description based on principal meridians (lines of longitude) and baselines (lines of latitude). Also called the *government survey system*.

redemption period the statutory period of time during which an owner can reclaim foreclosed property by paying the debt owed plus court costs and other charges established by statute.

redlining the illegal practice of lending institutions refusing to provide certain financial services, such as mortgage loans, to property owners in certain areas.

refinance transaction the process of paying off one loan with the proceeds from a new loan using the same property as security or collateral.

Regulation Z a Federal Reserve regulation that implements the federal Truth-in-Lending Act.

Real Estate Investment Trust (REIT) a public company that owns and often operates income-producing real estate. Some REITs also finance real estate.

release clause a clause in a mortgage that releases a portion of the property upon payment of a portion of the loan.

remainder estate a future interest in an estate that takes effect upon the termination of a life estate.

remainderman a person entitled to take an estate in remainder. For example, Louis grants a life estate to Marla that will pass to Shana upon Marla's death. Shana is the remainderman.

remaining balance in a mortgage, the amount of principal that has not yet been repaid.

remaining term the original amortization term minus the number of payments that have been applied to it.

rent a periodic payment paid by a lessee to a landlord for the use and possession of leased property.

replacement cost the estimated current cost to replace an asset similar or equivalent to the one being appraised.

reproduction cost the cost of building an exact duplicate of a building at current prices.

rescission canceling or terminating a contract by mutual consent or by the action of one party on default by the other party.

restriction (restrict covenant) a limitation on the way a property can be used.

return on equity (ROE) a measure of profitability relative to the amount of money shareholders have invested; calculated as net income divided by shareholders' equity.

return on investment (ROI) the ratio of money gained or lost on an investment relative to the amount of money invested; to calculate ROI, the return is divided by the amount invested.

reversion the return of interest or title to the grantor of a life estate.

reversionary interest a person has a reversionary interest in land when he or she has a right to take back property that he or she granted to another. For example, a landlord has a reversionary interest in leased property to take back possession at the termination of the lease. Here's another example: Gerry grants a life estate to Jessika that will revert back to Gerry upon Jessika's death. The person, Gerry in this case, is holding the reversionary right.

reverse annuity mortgage an agreement in which a homeowner receives monthly checks or a lump sum with no repayment until the property is sold; usually between a mortgagor and elderly homeowners.

revision a revised or new version, as in a contract.

right of egress (or ingress) the right to enter or leave designated premises.

right of first refusal the right of a person to have the first opportunity to purchase property before it is offered to anyone else.

right of redemption the statutory right to reclaim ownership of property after a foreclosure sale.

right of survivorship in joint tenancy, the right of survivors to acquire the interest of a deceased joint tenant.

riparian rights the rights of a landowner whose property is adjacent to a flowing waterway, such as a river, to access and use the water.

▶ S

safety clause a contract provision that provides a time period following expiration of a listing agreement, during which the agent will be compensated if there is a transaction with a buyer who was initially introduced to the property by the agent.

sale-leaseback a transaction in which the owner sells improved property and, as part of the same transaction, signs a long-term lease to remain in possession of its premises, thus becoming the tenant of the new owner.

sales contract a contract between a buyer and a seller outlining the terms of the sale.

salesperson one who is licensed to sell real estate in a given territory.

salvage value the value of a property at the end of its economic life.

satisfaction an instrument acknowledging that a debt has been paid in full.

second mortgage a mortgage that is in less than first lien position; see *junior mortgage.*

section as used in the rectangular survey system, an area of land measuring one square mile, or 640 acres.

secured loan a loan that is backed by property or collateral.

security property that is offered as collateral for a loan.

seisin the possession of a freehold estate in land by a person having the title.

seller carryback a means of owner financing whereby the owner lends the buyer the money—often as a second mortgage in combination with an assumed mortgage.

selling broker the broker who secures a buyer for a listed property; the selling broker may be the listing agent, a subagent, or a buyer's agent.

separate property property owned individually by a spouse, as opposed to community property.

servient tenement a property on which an easement or right-of-way for an adjacent (dominant) property passes.

setback the amount of space between the lot line and the building line, usually established by a local zoning ordinance or restrictive covenants; see *deed restrictions.*

settlement statement (HUD-1) the form used to itemize all costs related to closing of a residential transaction covered by RESPA regulations.

severalty the ownership of a property by only one legal entity.

shared appreciation mortgage (SAM) a fixed-rate, fixed-term loan that offers a lower interest rate in exchange for giving up a portion of the home's future value; can be up to 30-year mortgages.

sinking fund payment periodic payments that will accumulate by a specific future date to a specified future value.

special assessment a tax levied against only the specific properties that will benefit from a public improvement, such as a street or sewer; an assessment by a homeowners association for a capital improvement to the common areas for which no budgeted funds are available.

special warranty deed a deed in which the grantor guarantees the title only against the defects that may have occurred during the grantor's ownership and not against any defects that occurred prior to that time.

specific lien a lien, such as a mortgage, that attaches to one defined parcel of real estate.

specific performance a legal action in which a court compels a defaulted party to a contract to perform according to the terms of the contract, rather than awarding damages.

spread the difference between the asking price and the bid or the actual selling price.

standard payment calculation the method used to calculate the monthly payment required to repay the remaining balance of a mortgage in equal installments over the remaining term of the mortgage at the current interest rate.

state deed tax a transfer tax imposed on the value of real property transferred.

statute of frauds the state law that requires that certain contracts to be in writing in order to be enforceable.

statute of limitations the state law that requires that certain actions be brought to court within a specified period of time.

statutory lien a lien imposed on property by statute, such as a tax lien.

steering the illegal practice of directing prospective homebuyers to or away from particular areas.

straight-line depreciation a method of computing depreciation by decreasing value by an equal amount each year during the useful life of the property.

subdivision a tract of land divided into lots as defined in a publicly recorded plat that complies with state and local regulations.

sublet the act of a lessee transferring part or all of his or her lease to a third party while maintaining responsibility for all duties and obligations of the lease contract.

subject property a property for which a borrower is attempting to secure financing or refinancing; the property being appraised.

subordinate to voluntarily accept a lien position of lower priority than one to which one would normally be entitled.

substitution the principle in appraising that a buyer will be willing to pay no more for the property being appraised than the cost of purchasing an equally desirable property.

subrogation the substitution of one party into another's legal role as the creditor for a particular debt.

suit for possession a lawsuit filed by a landlord to evict a tenant who has violated the terms of the lease or retained possession of the property after the lease expired.

suit for specific performance a lawsuit filed for the purpose of compelling a party to perform particular acts to settle a dispute, rather than pay monetary damages.

survey a map that shows the exact legal boundaries of a property, the location of easements, encroachments, improvements, rights of way, and other physical features.

syndicate a group formed by a syndicator to combine funds for real estate investment.

▶ T

taxable value a percentage, after exemptions, of the assessor's appraisal according to a state-prescribed formula.

tax deed in some states, an instrument given to the purchaser at the time of sale.

tax lien a charge against a property created by law or statue. Tax liens take priority over all other types of liens.

tax rate the rate applied to the assessed value of a property to determine the property taxes.

tax sale the court-ordered sale of a property after the owner fails to pay *ad valorem* taxes owed on the property.

teaser rate a very low, temporary rate on an adjustable rate mortgage.

tenancy at sufferance the tenancy of a party who unlawfully retains possession of a landlord's property after the term of the lease has expired.

tenancy at will an indefinite tenancy that can be terminated by either the landlord or the tenant at any time by giving notice to the other party one rental period in advance of the desired termination date.

tenancy by the entirety ownership by a married couple of property acquired during the marriage with right of survivorship; not recognized by community property states.

tenancy in common a form of co-ownership in which two or more persons hold an undivided interest in property without the right of survivorship.

tenant one who holds or possesses the right of occupancy title.

tenement the space that may be occupied by a tenant under the terms of a lease.

term the length of a mortgage.

testate to die having created a valid will directing the testator's desires with regard to the disposition of the estate.

"time is of the essence" phrase in a contract that requires strict adherence to the dates listed in the contract as deadlines for the performance of specific acts.

time on the market the amount of time it takes a property to sell.

time sharing undivided ownership of real estate for only an allotted portion of a year.

time value of money the concept that money received now is worth more than the same rate in the future, even after adjusting for inflation, because money now can earn interest or other appreciation in that time.

title a legal document that demonstrates a person's right to, or ownership of, a property. **Note:** Title is *not* an instrument. The instrument, such as a deed, gives evidence of title or ownership.

title closing the transfer of ownership of property; the final step in a home sale, at which documents are signed and recorded.

title insurance an insurance policy that protects the holder from defects in a title, subject to the exceptions noted in the policy.

title search a check of public records to ensure that the seller is the legal owner of the property and that there are no liens or other outstanding claims.

Torrens system a system of registering titles to land with a public authority, who is usually called a registrar.

township a division of land, measuring 36 square miles, in the government survey system.

trade fixtures an item of personal property installed by a commercial tenant and removable upon expiration of the lease.

transfer tax a state or municipal tax payable when the conveyancing instrument is recorded.

trust an arrangement in which title to property is transferred from a grantor to a trustee, who holds title but not the right of possession for a third party, the beneficiary.

trustee a person who holds title to property for another person designated as the beneficiary.

Truth-in-Lending Law also known as Regulation Z; requires lenders to make full disclosure regarding the terms of a loan.

turnover the rate at which apartments are vacated.

▶ U

underwriting the process of evaluating a loan application to determine the risk involved for the lender.

undivided interest the interest of co-owners to use of an entire property despite the fractional interest owned.

unilateral contract a one-sided contract in which one party is obligated to perform a particular act completely, before the other party has any obligation to perform.

unsecured loan a loan that is not backed by collateral or security.

useful life the period of time a property is expected to have economic utility.

usury the practice of charging interest at a rate higher than that allowed by law.

▶ V

VA-guaranteed loan a mortgage loan made to a qualified veteran that is guaranteed by the Department of Veterans Affairs.

vacancy and noncollection an estimated amount to be deducted from potential gross income when preparing a budget.

vacancy rate a measurement of gross rental income loss because of vacancy and noncollection of rent; expressed as total potential gross rental income divided by lost rental income.

valid contract an agreement that is legally enforceable and binding on all parties.

valuation estimated worth.

variance permission obtained from zoning authorities to build a structure that is not in complete compliance with current zoning laws. A variance does not permit a non-conforming use of a property.

vendee a buyer.

vendor a seller; the property owner.

village an incorporated minor municipality usually larger than a hamlet and smaller than a town.

void contract a contract that is not legally enforceable; the absence of a valid contract.

voidable contract a contract that appears to be valid but is subject to cancellation by one or both of the parties.

▶ W

waiver the surrender of a known right or claim.

warranty deed a deed in which the grantor fully warrants a good clear title to the property.

waste the improper use of a property by a party with the right to possession, such as the holder of a life estate.

will a written document that directs the distribution of a deceased person's property, real and personal.

wraparound mortgage a mortgage that includes the remaining balance on an existing first mortgage plus an additional amount. Full payments on both mortgages are made to the wraparound mortgagee who then forwards the payments on the first mortgage to the first mortgagee.

writ of execution a court order to the sheriff or other officer to sell the property of a debtor to satisfy a previously rendered judgment.

▶ Y

yield a rate of return on an investment.

▶ Z

zone an area reserved by authorities for specific use that is subject to certain restrictions.

zoning ordinance the exercise of regulating and controlling the use of a property in a municipality.

d2495